Journey *Through* Peaceful Meditations

P.D. Archable

Journey *Through* Peaceful Meditations

Printed in the United States of America

Packaged by WinePress Publishing, PO Box 428, Enumclaw, WA 98022. The views expressed or implied in this work do not necessarily reflect those of WinePress Publishing. The author(s) is ultimately responsible for the design, content and editorial accuracy of this work.

ISBN 1-57921-537-8
Library of Congress Catalog Card Number: 2002116000

"You are my hiding place . . .
I will trust in You."

Dedication

This book is dedicated to many people: the Lord, who is my constant friend; my parents, Bonnie and Beulah Archable, who both went to be with the Lord in 2001; my son CJ, my daughter, Maisha, and all my family. I love you guys.

This book is also dedicated to those who have been struggling with the questions and problems of life. May these scriptures of peace bring hope, comfort, and joy to your hearts.

Acknowledgments

My eternal gratefulness to my Lord—my faithful Friend, devoted Father, all-powerful God. He has proven to be the essence of beauty and love, sweet music to my soul, the poet of eternity, and the author and finisher of my faith. He has been an indescribable source of comfort and grace in my life.

Special thanks to my very gifted daughter, Maisha Walker, for all her assistance and support.

Special thanks also to my dear friends Barbara Johnson, Joyce Joyner-Howell, Dru Moore, Marianne & Charles Matsuda, Kristin Fairbairn, and Ann Debban for believing in, encouraging, and providing me with a platform to allow my gifts to grow. I love you all.

Thank you to my sisters, Crystal Archable and Beverly Archable-Morrisey, for reviewing specific sections for editorial clarity.

My deepest gratitude to a very special pastor, Dr. Paul Risser, who showed me the tender love and mighty strength of Jesus. It was through your ministry that I gained eternal friendships with people like Ralph Litton and Ann Fisher who lavished upon me God's unconditional amazing love.

Contents

Preface

Have you ever wondered what life would be like without wars and conflicts? Have you ever wondered what life would be like without trouble or pain? Have you ever dreamed about how life would be without unforeseen events tearing at your very soul? It's a life we all long for, because life seems to hold much pain and sorrow.

But I wonder if I would appreciate the sanctity of life, relationships, and good times as much as I do if I had not experienced physical and emotional pain. I wonder what I would be like had not betrayal, disappointments, and failures occurred in my life.

One of my most frequent quotes is "Life is interesting." Simple words, but what does it mean? *Webster's Dictionary* defines interesting as "exciting curiosity or attention." Life is interesting because a situation can be looked at by different people in different ways. People will interpret and respond to an event differently because of the voices in their subconscious.

Life is interesting because on any given day, a crisis occurs in someone's life. On any given day a baby is born. On any given day a person dies. Someone is loved and someone is hated. The following week, the person who was loved is hated, and the person who was hated is loved. What fickle people we are. Why does it seem, at times, to take a crisis to bring about a united group? Why does it take a crisis to stir us to respect others and to listen to what another has to say? Ah, the flaws of humanity. The stories are similar; the people are different.

But how does one make sense of this passage called life? Sometimes we can't. Sometimes I feel a lot like the preacher in the Book of Ecclesiastes who stated, "Vanity of vanities, all is vanity . . . There is nothing new under the sun . . . Let us hear the conclusion of the whole matter: Fear God and keep His commandments, for this is the whole duty of man. For God will bring every work into judgment, including every secret thing, whether it is good or whether it is evil" (Eccles. 1:2, 9; 12:13–14 NKJV).

Some may ask, "Is that what life boils down to? After we are born, we are thrust into a world marked by geographical boundaries, full of people. Some acting without restraint among those who use perhaps too much restraint, and at the end—judgment?"

The answer to that question depends upon what type of lens you are looking through. Could the lens be blurred because of suffering hardships or getting one's way so easily? After all, we didn't ask to be born. We're thrown into a world full of uncertainties. Then we are judged. So the question of why life produces much pain and sorrow continues to float through time—different people asking the same question.

Perhaps the preacher's conclusion is not as cruel as some may interpret. I admit, I have a fear of God. But it's a reverence, a respect of One I view as loving and gracious. It's an understanding that the One I love and respect, who existed before this earth was created, possesses the intelligence and wisdom that we only catch a glimpse of. This loving God, who provides for and sustains us, desires that we all come to a knowledge of truth, for the truth makes us free.

Life requires that we seek out wisdom, knowledge, and truth. God Himself says, "My people perish for lack of knowledge" (Hos. 4:6). He exhorts us to study the Scriptures (2 Tim. 2:15). Some may bark at this exhortation, but is it unreasonable to implore your creation to seek out wisdom and truth that it may live abundantly? And, how does one measure abundant living? Is it measured only by material possessions? If so, then why can't we take those possessions with us after our departure from this world?

I propose that abundant living is connected to relationships and involves spiritual and soulish progression. I believe what the Bible says—that man possesses a spirit and soul. Even if we did not ask to be born, a responsibility is placed upon us to seek wisdom. We are accountable to one another and to God.

But is it such a bad thing? It's like a check and balance system. It's a way of striving toward peaceful, harmonious living. I share the psalmist's viewpoint that I'd rather live a humble, nonextravagant life than to live a life of material wealth reeking of discord, deceit, and vanity. Better still, "I'd rather be a doorkeeper in the house of my God than dwell in the tents of the wicked" (Ps. 84:10).

Call me nuts or small-minded, but "I know my Redeemer lives." Life experiences have taught me that God is available when I need Him. I have seen Him use the little of what I had and make it stretch. I have seen Him take a horrid situation and provide a way of escape. I have seen Him take the pain of betrayal and replace it with His comfort, understanding, and healing.

This is the God I know, and this is the God I want to share with others. He may not be understood, but He's just. He may not be appreciated, but He's gracious. He may not be revered, but He's merciful regardless. He does not react to our perceptions of Him. He is love, and He is who He says He is. When we are faced with pain, He heals us. When we are faced with discord, He releases peace. When hate is incited against us, He infuses His love. He's the God deserving of reverence, love, and commitment—the only true and living God.

Introduction

Achieving inner peace and serenity that sustains us during hard times does not come easily. Most of us have been taught to think the worst, worry, and brace ourselves for a shocker. Somehow, if the situation proves better than we anticipated, we are "one up" over the situation.

If you are anything like me, stealing away moments to be with God requires discipline. Attaining a level of unwavering peace during rough times requires focused meditation on His Word. Real peace does not come about through distracted mechanisms such as a great movie or "hitting the bottle." Real peace comes about through experiences and reminders of the victories God has given us. Real peace comes about through setting attentive, worshipful hearts on our Maker and His Word.

I once heard a pastor state, "A gap exists between God's promises and our circumstances, and we must fill that gap with faith (in God)." It made a lot of sense to me because many people question why the promises of God don't manifest in an astronomical way in their own lives. Certainly God has endowed us all with the potential to do great things. Great things don't particularly mean having a television show or becoming a millionaire. Jesus Himself says that a man's life doesn't consist in the abundance of his possessions (Luke 12:15b). We do great things when we fulfill the assignments God has given us individually, and those individual assignments contribute to the good of the whole.

How then can we allow God's promises to manifest more powerfully in our lives? We need to know what they are through the study of God's Word. We need to affirm them daily so that our eyes will be enlightened to what He has done for us and has in store for us.

We also need to look at what we really believe. We all have a belief system that determines how we think, feel, and respond to situations. Our belief system is our faith system. We either operate from a negative or positive faith system. In other words, our underlying mindset determines our circumstances. Are we filled with unbelief concerning God's promises? Are we lackadaisical or filled with disobedience regarding His principles? When we affirm God's promises, faith in who He is and what He can do rises in us.

You might ask, "How do we affirm those promises?" We affirm God's promises not by simply repeating them. We affirm His promises by meditating upon them, declaring them, applying them, and obeying His principles. It's a process. We begin by declaring, and we transcend to the desired effect through affirming. We can say that our actions are our affirmations. We must remember that faith without works produces nothing. We must put our faith in God's Word into action. We must have the God kind of faith. Meditating upon and applying His Word, which is good, virtuous, and true, serves as a catalyst for His promises to yield peaceful and fruitful living.

For centuries, many have used affirmations and meditations to actualize their potential and to manifest the greatness of God in their lives. It is not uncommon to find successful people who affirm on a regular basis. King David affirmed God's goodness throughout the day. Just read some of his psalms. They record some of the things he said and did to maintain a close relationship with God and to achieve major victories.

What about others in the Bible like Daniel who was known for his morning and noonday prayers? Daniel 9:4–19 gives us a clear picture of this man affirming God's nature and character during one of his prayers. After Paul's conversion, he neither ate nor drank for three days and was in constant prayer before the Lord—and, he did what God told him to do.

How about the greatest motivator of all times—Jesus Christ? He too meditated upon and spoke God's Word, and He was obedient even unto death. His obedience resulted in a glorious resurrection made available to every person. Jesus Christ continually told His disciples to remember His promises, have faith, and study and obey His Word. We have been given the greatest book in the world to learn from—the Bible. It's a book that gives us insight into the very nature of our Creator and His promises. Let's use it to our advantage.

How to Use This Book

Educators know that the more senses we involve in our learning process, the better we can assimilate the information. When I was in college, I practiced a study method many educators recommend. I read, highlighted, wrote, rewrote, repeated out loud, and meditated upon the study material provided by my professors. It helped me tremendously. Using that method allowed me to learn the material much more quickly than just reading the material alone. To assist the reader in attaining the peace God desires for us, I have included sections that incorporate the use of that method. These sections include:

Scriptures to learn what God is saying to us.
Stories to reinforce the meaning of selected scriptures.
Brief discussions of selected scriptures.
Daily prayers.
Meditation selections of companion scriptures.
Daily exercises that allow us to explore and verbally affirm how God is working in our lives and others.
Journal pages that can be used for completion of the exercises, written dialogue with the Lord, and application of the meditations.
Appendix A containing names, titles, and descriptions of God.
Appendix B containing personal declarations for use in your prayer time.

Appendix C containing God's promises.
Appendix D containing God's principles.

Morning and evening meditations provide a great way of starting and ending the day. The morning meditations in this book contain the daily scriptures with a brief discussion and some stories. The evening meditations contain the names, titles, definitions, and descriptions of God. For each evening meditation, review and meditate upon the name, title, or description of God. You may want to make statements out of the titles or descriptions of God. By doing this you infuse power into your thoughts and heart. When we verbally express who God is and what He can do, our confidence in Him becomes stronger and more secure. The Word of God says, "Death and life are in the power of the tongue" (Prov. 18:21 NKJV). Let's choose life by affirming all that He is. Read the companion scriptures (note: the scripture of the day is highlighted), and do the exercises below.

It also helps to select a memory verse. You may choose your own or use the scripture of the day. Confessing, writing, and rewriting the scripture will aid in memorizing it. (Another method in helping you to memorize your selected verses is to set aside two days of the week to use as a review of all your memory verses for the previous five days rather than starting a new devotion for those two days.)

Journalize on the opposite page, and write down any biblical promises and principles you find in the selected scriptures. Also, write out how you can apply what you have studied to your everyday life. Promise means to pledge, guarantee, or obligate oneself. God's promises are the things that He has given us in His Word to perform on our behalf. God's principles are His standards of conduct, instructions, and laws. Application of the devotion is putting into practice what we have learned. Before you complete your devotional time, close in praise, worship, and prayer.

One word about prayer—prayer can be very simple. It doesn't have to be elaborate or verbose. It doesn't have to sound religious or be filled with "Christianese." God looks at our hearts, and He says we are to worship Him in spirit and truth. Just approach Him ever so humbly. Jesus said, "And when you pray, do not keep on babbling like pagans, for they think they will be heard because of their many words. Do not be like them, for your Father knows what you need before you ask him" (Matt. 6:7–8). In Matthew 6:9, Jesus provides a good outline of prayer. It would be good to search through the Bible to see how others prayed. In praying the Scriptures, you add ammunition to your prayers because you are speaking the Word of God back to Him.

Whichever way you chose to use the book, I believe it will bring peace and comfort through unsettling times. Let's get started on this journey of peaceful meditations.

HORN OF SALVATION

RIGHTEOUSNESS

GLORIOUS MAJESTY

ANCIENT OF DAYS

KING OF ALL ETERNITY

DAY 1

God Helps Us During Troubling Times

Morning

God is our refuge and strength, an ever-present help in trouble. Therefore we will not fear, though the earth give way and the mountains fall into the heart of the sea, though its waters roar and foam and the mountains quake with their surging . . . The Lord Almighty is with us; the God of Jacob is our fortress.

(Ps. 46:1–3; 11)

Rely on God's System

Life holds many uncertainties. We were severely reminded of that fact by the tragic attacks of September 11, 2001, killing thousands of people when hijacked airline carriers plunged into the New York World Trade Center Towers, the Pentagon, and a field in Somerset County, Pennsylvania. It was a harsh reality for some Americans that we can no longer depend on systems of men. Nor can we any longer ignore the fears that other nations have been exposed to for years, even centuries. Our own backyard has been touched by the horrors of those who hate us—many of them faceless, many of them elusive. Other nations, seeing the impact of those horrible attacks, felt a reinforcement of their own reality.

But we can be assured that God, who has been hiding, saving, and delivering His very own people for centuries, will do the same for us. As we continue to humble ourselves and call upon His help, our fears will subside. We will gain the assurance that whatever happens in this physical realm will not harm our eternal heritage in Him.

Prayer

Father, help me draw close to You that I may experience Your peace in the midst of trouble. You are a very present help in times of trouble. I am grateful that Your complete peace is available to me. Your Word says that Your peace transcends my own understanding. Fill me and surround me with Your peace even now. I am comforted knowing that the Lord is my helper. I will not be seized with alarm or be terrified, for what can man do to me? Thank You, Lord, for the eternal heritage I have in You.

Evening

Refuge: A place of protection, to flee to; abode.

The Lord is a refuge for the oppressed, a stronghold in times of trouble.

(Ps. 9:9)

You evildoers frustrate the plans of the poor, but the Lord is their refuge.

(Ps. 14:6)

Free me from the trap that is set for me, for you are my refuge.

(Ps. 31:4)

Psalm 46:1–3, 11

____

____

____

____

____

____

____

____

____

> But I will sing of your strength, in the morning I will sing of your love; for you are my fortress, my refuge in times of trouble.
>
> (Ps. 59:16)

Exercise

Read Psalm 46. What does Psalm 46 tell you about God's nature? Close your eyes and think about how the Lord holds you securely during a difficult situation. Do not open your eyes until you sense His peace. Journalize your thoughts. List some things you can do to bring about peace under stressful circumstances (i.e. meditate on a psalm, play worship music).

Journal Exercise

Promise: ______________________________

Principle: ______________________________

Application: ______________________________

DAY 2

The Lord Keeps Me Safe

Morning

The Lord is my light and my salvation; whom shall I fear? The Lord is the strength of my life; of whom shall I be afraid? When the wicked, even mine enemies and my foes came upon me to eat up my flesh, they stumbled and fell. Though an host should encamp against me, my heart shall not fear; though war should rise against me in this will I be confident. One thing have I desired of the Lord, that I will seek after; that I may dwell in the house of the Lord all the days of my life to behold the beauty of the Lord and to inquire in his temple. For in the time of trouble, he shall hide me in his pavilion; in the secret of his tabernacle shall he hide me; he shall set me up upon a rock.

(Ps. 27:1–5 KJV)

Trudy's Deception

"What do you mean I'm fired?" Trudy asked in disbelief.

"Trudy, we simply don't need your services anymore," Katlyn stated. "We're streamlining the organization, and it was decided to eliminate your position."

"Eliminate my position? I was the one who brought in all the new accounts when you were floundering, Katlyn," said Trudy. "I taught you how to network and strategize . . ."

"Yes," interrupted Katlyn. "I really appreciate all you've done."

"So this is how I'm treated? You promised me partnership!" Trudy said angrily.

"Trudy, you'll be fine. It's just that I don't need you anymore. You understand, don't you? You're a smart woman. Besides, I'm sure you'll have no problem finding another job," Katlyn smirked.

"No, Katlyn," said Trudy. "This is not right."

"Look," said Katlyn, "I can make this very difficult for you. I can produce a document showing how you tampered with the sales figures on four different accounts."

"What?" shouted Trudy. "You know I'd never do anything like that. Katlyn, you know me."

Katlyn responded coldly, "I said I *could* produce such a document. I can send it to every board member."

"Katlyn, would you stoop to that?" Trudy asked incredulously.

"Get over it," Katlyn said. "Look, I have a meeting in about five minutes. You need to leave."

That night Trudy had trouble sleeping. The conversation with Katlyn continued to play in her mind. *How could she do this to me?* she asked herself. She began to cry. "Lord, help me," she prayed as tears continued to flow. As she closed her eyes, scriptures began to float through her mind about God's salvation and protection. *I know it will take time to work through the pain, but I have God's assurance that He will protect and heal me,* she thought. She then reached toward the nightstand and grabbed her Bible.

No matter what type of support we have from friends and relatives, sometimes we can still feel all alone in troubling situations. That is why some people end up taking their own lives. They just want to hide or check out. Instead of retreating within, we can "hide under the shadow of His wings." We can all take comfort in the salvation of the Lord. Let's take shelter in His tabernacle and allow Him to shower us with peace in His dwelling place.

Prayer

Father, I thank You for Your hiding place of safety. I thank You that I am never alone for You are always by my side. Thank You, Lord, for Your salvation. I ask now that You fill me with Your love, peace, and forgiveness. Father, I choose to forgive those who have hurt me. I will put away all bitterness, wrath, and evil speaking against others. I refuse to be offended or bitter because bitterness defiles many. Help me in this. I know that whatever I ask in the name of Jesus, I shall receive. I embrace the beauty of Your ways, my Lord. I love You.

Evening

Horn of my Salvation/Salvation: The one who makes safe, defends, delivers, and removes someone from a burden, oppression, or danger whereby victory is rendered. The one who preserves a person from spiritual suffering and death.

> My God is my rock, in whom I take refuge, my shield and the horn of my salvation. He is my stronghold, my refuge and my savior—from violent men you save me.
>
> (2 Sam. 22:3)

> The Lord is my rock, my fortress and my deliverer; my God is my rock, in whom I take refuge. He is my shield and the horn of my salvation, my stronghold.
>
> (Ps. 18:2)

Psalm 27:1–5

He alone is my rock and my salvation; he is my fortress, I will never be shaken.

(Ps. 62:2)

Behold, God is my salvation, I will trust and not be afraid; For Yah, the Lord, is my strength and song; He also has become my salvation.

(Isa. 12:2 NKJV)

Exercise

Think of a time when you were in a tight situation and received help when you least expected it. How did you respond? Thank the Lord for how He has helped you in the past. Tell the Lord how He can help you presently. Invite God's will and peace into your situation and thank Him for His intervention.

Journal Exercise

Promise: ______________________________

Principle: ______________________________

Application: ______________________________

DAY 3

Don't Be Afraid

Morning

But Jesus immediately said to them. Take courage! It is I. Don't be afraid.

(Matt. 14:27)

Do You Really Want Jesus' Help?

In my experience of working with homeless individuals, I saw many people reject the help that was offered them. The mission I worked for provided a lovely home to house women coming off drugs. During my earlier days, I was surprised that women actually left that home and returned to living on the streets. I had much to learn about the mentality of those who had become accustomed to living in rat-infested streets and alleys that often reeked of human waste.

After a while, I became more familiar with some of the thought processes and the games that accompanied drug addiction. When I walked the streets of skid row and was approached by an individual wanting money for food, I offered to provide food or point them in the direction of a mission that provided food. I would not give them money. How do you think they responded? Many refused the food. They wanted the money instead.

Unfortunately the minds of those individuals became blind and resistant to the help that was available to them. Their fears and refusal to look at truth kept them from moving forward. Many carried baggage from their past, and the drugs distorted their thinking. The streets had become their home. They felt no one could relate to their problems and preferred to live among those who shared their common thoughts and desires. Living on the streets became their comfort zone, and many did not want to accept the love Jesus offered them. They wanted to do things their own way. Sadly, doing things their own way kept them defeated. If only they had accepted His help.

All was not hopeless, though. Some did accept the help Jesus offered. It was not easy for those who accepted His help, but as they began to apply God's Word in their lives, constructive behavior replaced the self-destructive habits. It was a joy to see their lives changed by the power of God's Word.

If we can look past all the baggage, and the stained windows of our lives, we would see that Jesus is right here to help. If we cry out, His response is on the way. So what do you need from Him? Just ask.

Prayer

Lord, I thank You that You are always available to help. Even as You helped Your disciples when they were in the boat and thought they were sinking, You will help me. Sometimes it feels as if I am sinking. I realize that my problems appear much bigger than they really are. Help me to see Your bigness, and help me to see the smallness of my problems in comparison to You. Your Word says that perfect love casts out fear. You have not given me the spirit of fear, but You have given me power, love, and a sound mind. Remove any stains on my soul that have left my perception of situations or You distorted. I cast my care upon You, for You care for me. I thank You for Your help.

Evening

Strength: Powerful, mighty, wealthy, never-failing, eternal, courageous, victorious, forceful; the ability to perform in battle; the ability to make wealthy.

Help: Deliverance, aid, protection, relief, assistance.

The Lord is my strength and my shield; my heart trusts in him, and I am helped.
(Ps. 28:7)

I was pushed back and about to fall, but the Lord helped me. The Lord is my strength and my song; he has become my salvation.

(Ps. 118:13–14)

Rescue: Make safe; free; to be snatched.

He brought me out into a spacious place; he rescued me because he delighted in me.

(Ps. 18:19)

Matthew 14:27

____

____

____

____

Exercise

Is there a situation in your life that you are not allowing God to help you with? What is keeping you from accepting His help? Why does Jesus exhort us to take courage and not fear? Read the following scriptures: Matt. 10:31; Lk. 8:50; Lk. 12:32; and Isa 41:10. What message does God want to get across? What are the different areas God wants to heal and provide for?

Journal Exercise

Promise: ______________________________

Principle: ______________________________

Application: ______________________________

DAY 4

God Resurrects and Gives Me Life

Morning

> I am the resurrection and the life. He who believes in me will live, even though he dies, and whoever lives and believes in me will never die. Do you believe this?
>
> (John 11:25–26)

Embracing Eternal Life

Believing that Jesus is the resurrection and life takes faith. Actually it takes childlike faith because the question He asks in John 11:26 challenges our logic. Perhaps believing Jesus is the resurrection and life was easy for me because I learned about Him as a child. How happy I was to learn that this loving God would want me to live forever with Him. As I became older and was faced with the logic of man, my belief that Jesus is the resurrection did not waver, although other facets of my faith wavered. After all, I remember talking to Him as a child. I knew He was listening, and I wanted the abiding life He offered.

God assures us that those who embrace the abiding life of Jesus won't taste death. God will keep us through any situation. In order to enter into this eternal rest, one must believe that He is and that He rewards those who diligently seek Him. On one occasion

Jesus told the multitude, "When a man believes in me, he does not believe in me only, but in the one who sent me. When he looks at me, he sees the one who sent me. I have come into the world as a light, so that no one who believes in me should stay in darkness" (John 12:44–46). Sometimes we need to be like the man in Mark 9:24 who said to Jesus, "I do believe; help me overcome my unbelief."

Prayer

Father, I embrace the abiding life of Jesus. I know that Jesus is everything I will ever need for any situation and that He rewards those who diligently seek Him. Father, I am running hard after Jesus. Help me to overcome any unbelief. I realize that even if my faith is as small as a mustard seed, it is enough for Your power to work in my life. Thank You for the measure of faith You have given me. Thank You for the abiding life of Jesus in me.

Evening

Resurrection: Resurgence from death; rising from death.

John 11:25–26

____

____

____

Life/Life-giving: Vitalize; spirit, soul, heart, and mind vitality; existence; make alive.

Jesus answered, "I am the way and the truth and the life. No one comes to the Father except through me. If you really knew me, you would know my Father as well. From now on, you do know him and have seen him."

(John 14:6–7)

We know also that the Son of God has come and has given us understanding, so that we may know him who is true. And we are in him who is true—even in his Son Jesus Christ. He is the true God and eternal life.

(1 John 5:20)

Breath of life: Wind; life spirit.

But after the three and a half days a breath of life from God entered them, and they stood on their feet, and terror struck those who saw them.

(Rev. 11:11)

Exercise

What does resurrection mean to you? How does it affect your eternal existence? What is your assurance that you have eternal life?

Journal Exercise

Promise: ______________________________

Principle: ______________________________

Application: ______________________________

DAY 5

The Divine Promise of the Covenant Keeper

Morning

> Blessed is the man who perseveres under trial, because when he has stood the test, he will receive the crown of life that God has promised to those who love him.
>
> (James 1:12)

The Instructions

Helen was tired, but she managed to find her way through the dusty, crooked stairway into a lighted waiting area. She had not seen anyone since she arrived at the town of Nissi. Only empty cars lined the landscaped streets. She read the note again to make sure she was following all the instructions carefully. After having made quite a few dreadful mistakes, she wanted to be certain she was on the right course. She had become discouraged and almost ready to quit after the last incident.

"Well, I did take the right turn that time," she said aloud. "Oh, there's the Manor House I am to go to. At last," she sighed, "my final clue."

She opened the door and found the lobby empty. She proceeded up the dark stairway. Once inside the lighted waiting area, she reached into her pocket for the instructions. They read, "Be seated until someone comes for you."

This will be my opportunity to finally talk to another person. What a strange, yet exciting journey it's been, she thought.

Just then the door opened, but she didn't see anyone.

"Enter please," a voice said.

She got up nervously from her chair. As she started through the door, she felt an eerie presence gently shoving a card into her hand. A gentle, dignified elderly man stood in the other room.

"Welcome, Helen," he said. "I see you made it safely. You apparently followed the instructions precisely."

"I . . . well . . . I did study the training manual, cover to cover. Coming here has been my life's dream," Helen said.

"You did well, Helen. Quite well. I'll take the card. By the way, my name is Mr. Sleaver," he smiled.

"But I was to ask for a Mr. Nissi," said Helen.

"I am sorry, but he is not able to make it. He sent me to greet you instead. Your next and last assignment requires that you leap from the top of this building into your final destination. Take my hand. I will escort you."

Something is not right, Helen thought.

"Is something wrong? I can assure you, it will be quite safe," Mr. Sleaver said. "You've always been protected during your journey, haven't you?" he smiled.

"Leave me now!" she shouted.

"Think it over," he said. "You will need me later."

"No, thank you. Now go," she said calmly.

She went back into the outer room and waited in her seat. She thought about everything that had occurred and remembered the warning about imposters approaching her during her journey. As she was pondering those thoughts, another man appeared at the door.

"Are you ready?" he asked.

"Is there a Mr. Nissi here?" she asked.

"Yes," he answered. "Come right on in." He led her into another room. The walls were lined with golden bins that were filled with beautiful gifts.

"I have a room reserved in the name of Helen Campbell," she told the clerk.

"Let's see. Oh, yes," he said. "Your name is written here. I am glad you made it through. You can redeem this card for your reward," he smiled.

The Bible tells us, "God is not a man, that he should lie, nor a son of man, that he should change his mind" (Num. 23:19). In other words, He keeps His promises to us. We can depend on Him and trust Him to carry out the promises He has made to us. What a good feeling to know that there is a crown of life for those who love God and stand faithful to His ways to the very end.

Prayer

Father, when I am discouraged about conflicts and trouble in my life, help me to realize that You are always there for me. Father, I present my problems to you, knowing that You will help me. Father, I will not give in to any wrong temptations; I will pursue integrity in my dealings; I will continue to keep You involved in my decisions because Your wisdom causes me to live in safety and be at ease without fear of harm. Thank You that, as I persevere under trial and stand faithful to Your ways, I will receive the crown of life.

Evening

Covenant-keeper: One who protects, maintains, and guards a devisory will, contract, a solemn binding agreement, promise, or testament.

> I will establish my covenant as an everlasting covenant between me and you and your descendants after you for the generations to come, to be your God and the God of your descendants after you.
>
> (Gen. 17:7)

> I prayed to the Lord my God and confessed: "O Lord, the great and awesome God, who keeps his covenant of love with all who love him and obey his commands, we have sinned and done wrong. We have been wicked and have rebelled; we have turned away from your commands and laws.
>
> (Dan. 9:4–5)

James 1:12

____

____

____

____

Reward: Future posterity; recompense; gift; prize.

After this, the word of the Lord came to Abram in a vision: "Do not be afraid, Abram. I am your shield, your very great reward."

(Gen. 15:1)

Exercise

Can you relate to Daniel's prayer above? What does it say about God? What does it say about man? What does God promise for those who love Him? What should you be focusing on when faced with trials?

Journal Exercise

Promise:

Principle:

Application:

DAY 6

You're Invited to the Wedding Supper of the Lamb

Morning

> "Hallelujah! For our Lord God Almighty reigns. Let us rejoice and be glad and give him glory! For the wedding of the Lamb has come, and his bride has made herself ready. Fine linen, bright and clean, was given her to wear . . ." Then the angel said to me, "Write: 'Blessed are those who are invited to the wedding supper of the Lamb.'" And he added, "These are the true words of God."
>
> (Rev. 19:6–9)

Clothing of the Saints

Hallelujah stands for an exuberant, jubilant praise to the Lord. We praise Him because of His sacrifice that resulted in our salvation. We also praise Him because He truly reigns over all. The only way that we know He reigns in us is to invite Him to be the Master of our lives. When we invite Him to be the essential part of our lives, He in turn invites us to be blessed by His generous love, care, and protection.

The goodness we experience on earth, however, cannot compare to the wedding supper of the Lamb. Revelation 19:7 speaks of those participating in the wedding supper of the Lamb. It reads "His bride [the church] has made herself ready." The type of clothing the bride is wearing gives us a clue as to how she is presented to the Lamb (Jesus

Christ). Fine linen represents the righteous acts of the saints. Bright represents the glory of the saints, and clean indicates that the blood of the Lamb has purified the bride. She is now free from corrupt desires and guilt.

And just who are the invited? The word *ready* is a crucial key. In Matthew 25:1–13, Jesus speaks of ten wise virgins and ten foolish virgins. Verse 10 says, "The [wise] virgins who were *ready* went in with him [the groom] to the wedding banquet. And the door was shut." Jesus admonishes us to keep watch since we don't know the day or hour of His return. He doesn't want any of us to be left behind. Let's persevere to apply God's ways to our lives so that we can sing, "Hallelujah, we are a ready bride for Jesus." Thank God for His gracious and merciful invitation.

Prayer

Father, what a great time of fellowship that awaits me at the wedding supper of the Lamb. How can I thank You enough for the invitation to dine with You and Your great family of believers? Your invitation brings me much joy. Count me in, Father, for that great wedding supper of the Lamb. Thank You, Lord.

Evening

Lamb: A gentle, innocent, or gullible person. The lamb symbolizes sacrificial surrendering. Jesus was called the Lamb because He willingly submitted to those who orchestrated his death. In the same way that sheep are led by shepherds and are said to follow the master's voice, Jesus willingly followed the voice of the Father despite the human pain and suffering He was to endure. His trust and knowledge of the Father was unshakable.

> . . . but with the precious blood of Christ, a lamb without blemish or defect. He was chosen before the creation of the world but was revealed in these last times for your sake.
>
> (1 Pet. 1:19–20)

In a loud voice they sang: "Worthy is the Lamb, who was slain, to receive power and wealth and wisdom and strength and honor and glory and praise."

(Rev. 5:12)

They will make war against the Lamb, but the Lamb will overcome them because he is Lord of lords and King of kings—and with him will be his called, chosen and faithful followers.

(Rev. 17:14)

Revelation 19:6–9

____

____

____

____

____

____

Exercise

How did Jesus develop an unshakable trust in the Father? Write down what it means to be invited to the wedding supper of the Lamb. Why do you think it is called wedding supper of the Lamb and not wedding supper of Rabboni or Christ? How should you prepare yourself for the wedding supper of the Lamb?

Journal Exercise

Promise: ______________________________

Principle: ______________________________

Application: ______________________________

DAY 7

What Are You Seeking from the Lord God Almighty?

Morning

Seek good, not evil, that you may live. Then the Lord God Almighty will be with you. (Amos 5:14)

The Choice

"Your time is up," said the ghostly figure. "You've had your chance to do good in this life. I came to you in various forms. You just wouldn't change. You could have helped the homeless person on Fifth and Walnut Street on November 9, 1995. You could have offered food to your aunt who lost her job in 1990. You could have taken your arthritic brother to his doctor appointments. You were always too busy," he said.

"But I'm no different from most people," Mr. Rippart retorted.

The ghostly figure continued.

"You didn't have to lie about your co-worker. You didn't have to harass your mother to change her will in your favor. You didn't have to fire that hard-working single mother in 1998. You know the one—Gloria."

"I still say I'm no different from most people."

"Listen," said the ghostly figure, raising his voice, "I didn't tell you to be like most people. Was it too hard to seek good? Was it really easier to do evil?" His voice then became very harsh and firm. "You refused to look at circumstances from an eternal perspective. You only cared about your temporary, shallow existence. You refused to show kindness to others. Your heart became cold and hardened to any suggestions of making a positive impact on the world around you. You made your choice and your time is up!"

Seeking God is a daily act. It is a continuum that should not be broken. When we rise in the morning, our gratefulness and dependence should turn to Him. As we go about our daily duties, we should turn our attention (even if silently) to acknowledge Him and ask for His guidance. During the evening as we watch the news, we should petition Him concerning what we see and hear on the television. Before we lay down to sleep, our thoughts should center on His loving care over our family, national leaders, and country. As you turn over during the night, reflect on His greatness and protection. Lean on His good ways always, meditate on Him, and surely the Lord God will be with you.

Prayer

Father, I do seek good. I am a seeker of Your heart. Your way is the path to life everlasting. Help me to always keep You in the forefront of my mind and in everything that I do. Keep me from evil so that I will not hurt others. I want You to be glorified in me.

EVENING

Presence: Face, favor, honor, countenance, glory, revelation, manifested authority.

The Lord replied, "My Presence will go with you, and I will give you rest."

(Exod. 33:14)

Blessed are those who have learned to acclaim you, who walk in the light of your presence, O Lord. They rejoice in your name all day long; they exult in your righteousness. For you are their glory and strength, and by your favor you exalt our horn.

(Ps. 89:15–17)

Amos 5:14

___

___

___

> May he strengthen your hearts so that you will be blameless and holy in the presence of our God and Father when our Lord Jesus comes with all his holy ones.
>
> (1 Thess. 3:13)

Exercise

List some of the changes you can incorporate so that the Lord's presence can be manifested in your life on a greater level.

Journal Exercise

Promise:

Principle:

Application:

DAY 8

The Rewards of Giving

Morning

Do not be deceived. God cannot be mocked. A man reaps what he sows. The one who sows to please his sinful nature, from that nature will reap destruction; the one who sows to please the Spirit, from the Spirit will reap eternal life. Let us not become weary in doing good, for at the proper time, we will reap a harvest if we do not give up.

(Gal. 6:7–9)

The Seeds

There once was a man named Jim who lived in a town with a population of about 200 people. The town was small enough that everyone knew each other. One summer the town experienced a drought, which affected the crops. The following year, food was scarce. Desperate people began stealing from each other.

One day, a wise woman came to the town, knocked on Jim's door, and told him she was sent to help. She opened a box that contained tiny, drought-resistant seeds. These seeds, she told him, would produce a crop in about one month. The only thing Jim had to do was to uproot ten new plants each month and distribute them among the townsfolk until each family received a plant. She told him that she would be back to check on him in six months.

Six months passed and the woman returned to the town. She was not surprised by what she saw. When she knocked on the door, a shriveled old man answered. "Jim," she said, "I see you didn't do as I instructed. You tried to keep everything for yourself, didn't you?" she asked.

"How did you know?" he asked with his head down.

"If you had shared what was given you, the entire area would have become fertile. If you decided to keep it all for yourself, not only would the area become more desolate, but you would accelerate in age. What I gave you was meant to bless everyone, not just yourself," she responded sadly.

Blessing others reaps many rewards. There are so many ways we can help in this world. Can you volunteer at a shelter? Do you have time to help a friend? Can you listen to someone who is trying to figure out what to do with his or her life? Can you love the unlovable? What about giving a hug to someone who needs to feel your comforting arms? There's always a need to provide money to buy food for hungry children or clothes for the destitute.

Whatever you give, God says, it will be returned to you in a greater measure. When we open our hands to help someone, it also acts as a reservoir to receive whatever comes back. The motive shouldn't be giving just to receive something in return. That type of giving serves selfish purposes. The principle of sowing and reaping tells us that we will receive when we give to others, however. What do you have to give? Mother Theresa was a perfect example of someone who gave her life for the benefit of others. She died a fulfilled woman, knowing that her return produced a much greater reward than the temporal, material things of this world.

Prayer

Father, You are the gracious God who is always working behind the scenes for our good. You give so lovingly to us. You stated in Your Word that you desire to give good gifts to Your children. Jesus tells us that "in everything, do to others what we would have them do to us." You desire that we invest what You have given us to produce more so that Your Will would be carried out in the earth. As we give to help others, good returns to us. Teach me more and more about Your principles of giving. I desire that the motivation behind my giving would be pleasing in Your sight. I pray that Your Will be carried out in this earth through the giving of my time, money, and love.

Evening

The Spirit: The breath; the life; the inmost part or essence of God.

The Spirit of the Sovereign Lord is on me, because the Lord has anointed me to preach good news to the poor. He has sent me to bind up the brokenhearted, to proclaim freedom for the captives and release from darkness for the prisoners, to proclaim the year of the Lord's favor, and the day of vengeance of our God, to comfort all who mourn.

(Isa. 61:1–2)

I urge you, brothers, by our Lord Jesus Christ and by the love of the Spirit, to join me in my struggle by praying to God for me.

(Rom. 15:30)

This is what we speak, not in words taught us by human wisdom but in words taught by the Spirit, expressing spiritual truths in spiritual words.

(1 Cor. 2:13)

Galatians 6:7–9

____

____

Exercise

Write down seven ways in which you can give to help others. How will you implement your giving? (Note: We sometimes become overly committed. Our commitments should not take away time that we should otherwise spend with God and our families.)

Journal Exercise

Promise:

Principle:

Application:

DAY 9

Power

Morning

> O Lord God of our fathers, are you not the God who is in heaven? You rule over all the kingdoms of the nations. Power and might are in your hand, and no one can withstand you . . . We do not know what to do, but our eyes are on you.
>
> (2 Chron. 20:6, 12)

Humility That Moves the Hand of God

King Jehoshaphat was a powerful man. Yet, when a difficult situation presented itself, he was not too proud to ask God for help. His humility and integrity before the Lord caused the Lord's hand to move swiftly on his behalf. The words, "We do not know what to do, but our eyes are on you," pulls at the very heart of God. God says that if His people who are called by His name will humble themselves and seek His face and turn from their wicked ways, then He will hear from heaven, forgive their sin, and heal their land (2 Chron. 7:14). Let us thank God for leaders who, like Jehoshaphat, rely on and trust Him. Let us humble ourselves before Him, confess our sins, and seek His ways.

Prayer

Father, I humble myself before You. Show me if there is any pride in my heart that hinders my relationship with You and others. Father, forgive me for placing a lesser value on prayer. I realize how important it is to be humble before You and to pray for the nation. Please help me to place praying for this nation and its leaders as a priority. You said that it pleases You when we intercede for everyone and those in authority. You desire that we do this so that we may live peaceful and quiet lives in all godliness and holiness. I ask that You hear my prayer of repentance and heal the land. I also pray that others would be awakened to pray regularly for our leaders and the nation. Your Word says that blessed is the nation whose God is the Lord.

Evening

Power/Powerful: Valor, victory, force, virtue, strength, ability, capable, miracle, might/operable.

The voice of the Lord is powerful; the voice of the Lord is majestic.

(Ps. 29:4)

The Lord reigns: Royal dominion; rule as king.

Let the heavens rejoice, let the earth be glad, let them say among the nations, "The Lord reigns!"

(1 Chron. 16:31)

God reigns over the nations; God is seated on his holy throne.

(Ps. 47:8)

2 Chronicles 20:6, 12

___

___

___

Exercise

Have you ever called on God to move in your life in a powerful way? What happened? In what way does God reign in your life? Have you given Him permission? If not, why not? How can you apply 2 Chronicles 20:6 to your own life?

Journal Exercise

Promise: ________________________________

Principle: ________________________________

Application: ________________________________

DAY 10

God is the Lead Warrior

Morning

> Give thanks to the Lord for his love endures forever. And as they began to sing and praise, the Lord set ambushes against [their enemies] and they were defeated.
> (2 Chron. 20:21b–22)

Praise in the Midst of Trouble

You may ask, "How can I sing and praise God when everything seems to be coming against me?" This principle regarding praise and worship is one of the paradoxes in the Bible. Yet story after story confirms the validity of what takes place when you praise God in the midst of trouble. Something wonderful and significant happens when we focus on what God is able to do for His covenanted people. We focus on the victory God can bring about rather than the troubling circumstances.

In the scripture you just read, God rescued Jehoshaphat and the people of Judah. What was the process of this great rescue? Jehoshaphat physically and emotionally humbled himself before the Lord. He confessed his weaknesses and then asked God for help. Afterwards, he believed, obeyed, and praised God for deliverance. It takes a humble attitude to believe and praise God. In contrast, a proud, self-reliant attitude tells God that His help is not wanted or needed. It actually closes the door to permanent victory. That's why it is important to remember that pride goes before destruction and a haughty spirit before a fall (Prov. 16:18). Let's continue to praise the Lord in good times and bad.

Prayer

Lord, I praise You for Your goodness and mercy. Your mercies are new every morning, and Your faithfulness is never ending. I choose to praise You in the midst of troubled times. I choose to trust You in the midst of conflict. I choose to trust You with all my needs. Please help me to see the many ways You are kind and merciful to me. No matter what, my heart will sing of Your mercies forever.

Evening

Lead warrior: Chief soldier or chief strategist.

The Lord will fight for you; you need only be still.

(Exod. 14:14)

The Lord is a warrior, the Lord is his name.

(Exod. 15:3)

For the Lord your God is the one who goes with you to fight for you against your enemies to give you victory.

(Deut. 20:4)

2 Chronicles 20:21b–22

> "Don't be afraid," the prophet answered. "Those who are with us are more than those who are with them." And Elisha prayed, "O Lord, open his eyes so he may see." Then the Lord opened the servant's eyes, and he looked and saw the hills full of horses and chariots of fire all around Elisha. As the enemy came down toward him, Elisha prayed to the Lord, "Strike these people with blindness." So he struck them with blindness, as Elisha had asked.
>
> (2 Kings 6:16–18)

Exercise

What do the above scriptures tell us about God's protection? How should we respond when faced with adverse circumstances?

Journal Exercise

Promise: ______________________________

Principle: ______________________________

Application: ______________________________

DAY 11

God Provides

Morning

Therefore, I tell you, do not worry about your life, what you will eat or drink; or about your body, what you will wear. Is not life more important than food, and the body more important than clothes? Look at the birds of the air, they do not sow or reap or store away in barns, and yet your heavenly Father feeds them. Are you not much more valuable than they? Who of you by worrying can add a single hour to his life? . . . But seek first his kingdom and his righteousness, and all these things will be given you as well. Therefore do not worry about tomorrow, for tomorrow will worry about itself. Each day has enough trouble of its own.

(Matt. 6:25–27; 33–34)

Leeches That Kill

She made her way to the front of the church for one last look at her aunt before they closed the casket. She tried to tell her aunt many times to enjoy herself. Her aunt felt she could no longer enjoy life. Her husband had left her penniless; her children lived in other states and were not interested in maintaining a relationship with her.

Carole did all she could to help her aunt. She had run errands for her. She even bought her groceries, knowing that her aunt had nothing to offer in return. "Still, family should stick together," Carole told her aunt. No matter what Carole said, her aunt continued to worry. The final straw came when her aunt was diagnosed with cancer. There was no cheering her up then. She simply gave up and died.

Worry, stress, and anxiety drain the very life out of us. They are leeches that kill us. Little by little, worry eats away at our physical and mental states. We worry about this event or that event, yet our worry doesn't help us solve the problem. We think that if we don't worry, we are not sensitive to what's going on in our lives. The irony is that many illnesses are brought on by stress. God tells us, however, to give the situation to Him and let Him carry the burden. He wants us to live a long and satisfying life. That is not such a bad exchange, is it?

Prayer

Lord, I thank You that You see me as valuable. I am grateful for Your reminder that You care about me. I don't have to worry about my life for it is in Your hands. I thank You that I can give You my problems in exchange for Your peace. I seek Your kingdom and Your righteousness, Lord. You will give me perfect peace as my mind meditates on Your ways, strength, and power. Thank You for Your promise that You have provided for me all that I will ever need.

Evening

Jehovah Jireh: Father provider; the one who sets up, prepares, establishes, and looks out for me beforehand.

> So Abraham called that place The Lord Will Provide. And to this day it is said, "On the mountain of the Lord it will be provided."
>
> (Gen. 22:14)

> I will provide for you there, because five years of famine are still to come. Otherwise you and your household and all who belong to you will become destitute.
>
> (Gen. 45:11)

> The wild animals honor me, the jackals and the owls, because I provide water in the desert and streams in the wasteland, to give drink to my people, my chosen, the people I formed for myself that they may proclaim my praise.
>
> (Isa. 43:20–21)

Matthew 6:25–34

___

___

___

___

___

___

___

___

___

___

___

Exercise

What does God promise for His chosen in Isaiah 43:20–21? How can you apply Matthew 6:25–34 to your circumstances? List ways in which Jehovah Jireh has provided for you.

Journal Exercise

Promise: ____

Principle: ____

Application: ____

DAY 12

Merciful God

Morning

Praise be to the Lord, for he has heard my cry for mercy. The Lord is my strength and my shield; my heart trusts in him, and I am helped. My heart leaps for joy and I will give thanks to him in song.

(Ps. 28:6–7)

The Judgment

She ran joyfully through the town, jumping, shouting, and shedding tears.

"What's all the commotion about?" Mrs. Freckles asked.

"It's Christina. Judge Copperfield exonerated her. She's a free woman," Charlene explained.

"What?" Mrs. Freckles asked in disbelief and anger. "Why, I know she's as guilty as sin. I'm sure she has no intentions of restoring the property she damaged. I'm sure that fire was no mistake. I take it all those phony tears paid off. That Judge Copperfield falls for anything."

"But, Mrs. Freckles," responded Charlene, "the judge is known to be fair and honest, a man who makes sound judgments."

"Sound? What's so sound about turning an arsonist loose?" Mrs. Freckles asked. "No one was in the house except Christina. She probably didn't get along with her mother," retorted Mrs. Freckles.

"I believe Christina's story, and more importantly, her mother believes her," said Charlene.

"Hah!" said Mrs. Freckles sarcastically. "That story about her tripping and knocking the oil lamp over?"

"Mrs. Freckles, you and I both know that Christina has always been good to her mother. I believe her," Charlene reiterated. "She suffered second-degree burns, and she lost the only home she has ever known. Should she be punished further?" Charlene asked. "Besides, Mrs. Freckles, she needs our help, not our judgment."

Many times we also need help, not judgment. Our God is a just God who makes Himself available to us. As we cry out for mercy, He hears us. Isn't it great that as we lean on Him, we become strong? *Vine's Dictionary* states that "mercy is the act of God, and peace is the resulting experience in man's heart." That peace, and the joy that comes with it, gives us strength to go on.

Prayer

Lord, at the voice of my cry You hear and answer me. Your mercy is from everlasting to everlasting and upon those who revere You. Thank You for being my strength and shield. Your unfailing love is my comfort. I will sing and give You praise, Lord, for You are good and merciful. Just as You protected others in difficult circumstances, You will protect me.

Evening

Merciful/Father of mercies: One who shows pity, favor, kindness, and compassion for the ills of others. The One who provides for atonement, covering.

> For the Lord your God is a merciful God; he will not abandon or destroy you or forget the covenant with your forefathers, which he confirmed to them by oath.
>
> (Deut. 4:31)

> But in your great mercy you did not put an end to them or abandon them, for you are a gracious and merciful God.
>
> (Neh. 9:31)

Psalm 28:6–7

____

____

____

____

____

> The Lord your God is merciful and forgiving, even though we have rebelled against him.
>
> (Dan. 9:9)

> Blessed be the God and Father of our Lord Jesus Christ, the Father of mercies and God of all comfort, who comforts us in all our tribulation, that we may be able to comfort those who are in trouble, with the comfort with which we ourselves are comforted by God.
>
> (2 Cor. 1:3–4 NKJV)

Exercise

Think about the different judges you see on television and read about in the newspaper. Do you believe they are always just in their dealings? Why? How would they compare to God the judge and discerner of hearts? How has God been merciful to you? In what ways has His mercy impacted your life? Is there someone in your life that you have been judging in a critical manner? What should your attitude be toward that person? How can you show mercy to that person?

Journal Exercise

Promise: ____

Principle: ____

Application: ____

DAY 13

Shepherd of My Soul

Morning

The Lord is the strength of his people, a fortress of salvation for his anointed one. Save your people and bless your inheritance. Be their shepherd and carry them forever.

(Ps. 28:8–9)

Make Him Your Shepherd

When I was laid off from my position at the mission, it could have been a frightening and devastating time for me. It wasn't. I didn't have a husband, friend, or relative who could provide me with an income to keep things afloat. I had a shepherd, however, who had promised to provide and care for me.

God had already prepared me before the layoff. I knew the mission was experiencing financial problems. During those times, fear gripped many who had no idea what the future held for them. We always wondered whose name would be on the layoff lists. Some thought I would not be laid off because I supervised the inner city outreach for women.

I remember one co-worker who feared being laid off. She was so sure that she would be among the unemployed. She was very surprise to learn that she would keep her job, and I was among those in the third group of layoffs.

Instead of fear gripping me, I experienced what the Bible calls "the peace that passes all understanding." I knew God had given me grace to bear up under the circumstances. Only once during that period of not having a job did fear try to creep in; but I attacked it immediately with the promise that God would provide for me. I continued to fight that fear until I felt His peace again.

God didn't miss a beat. By the time my severance pay ran out, another company hired me. The benefit package was much better than the one I had at the mission. My shepherd carried me then, and that situation gave me confidence to know that He will continue to carry me forever.

Let's not lose heart with the difficulties of life. The shepherd and overseer of our soul is more than able to meet our needs—and He doesn't miss a beat.

Prayer

Father, I thank You that You are the all-knowing and all-powerful God. It makes me feel confident having a Father who is wiser and more powerful than anything or anyone. You are my fortress and my salvation. I can run to You for safety. You are my shepherd and I shall not lack for anything. I am grateful for the grace that You give me to hold up under trying circumstances. Please continue to be my strength and carry me forever.

Evening

Shepherd: The one who tends to or leads a flock. God is our shepherd who tends to our physical, emotional, and spiritual needs.

> Then he blessed Joseph and said, "May the God before whom my fathers Abraham and Isaac walked, the God who has been my shepherd all my life to this day, the Angel who has delivered me from all harm—may he bless these boys."
>
> (Gen. 48:15–16a)

But his bow remained steady, his strong arms stayed limber, because of the hand of the Mighty One of Jacob, because of the Shepherd, the Rock of Israel, because of your father's God, who helps you, because of the Almighty, who blesses you with blessings of the heavens above, blessings of the deep that lies below, blessings of the breast and womb.

(Gen. 49:24–25)

The Lord is my shepherd, I shall not be in want.

(Ps. 23:1)

Psalm 28:8–9

____

____

____

____

I am the good shepherd. The good shepherd lays down his life for the sheep.

(John 10:11)

Exercise

How is God like a shepherd to you? Picture a shepherd carrying a helpless lamb. Now picture God as the shepherd and you as the lamb. Journalize your thoughts.

Journal Exercise

Promise:

Principle:

Application:

DAY 14

My Fortress

Morning

> He who dwells in the secret place of the Most High shall abide under the shadow of the Almighty. I will say of the Lord, "He is my refuge and my fortress; my God, in Him I will trust."
>
> (Ps. 91:1–2 NKJV)

My God in Whom I Trust

Have you ever wondered why God constantly implores us to trust Him? During my first year in college, I stayed on campus. I was extremely shy, but I managed to connect with a very special person. This new friend, Jamie, talked so much about the Lord that it drew me closer and closer to Him. We started praying together and sharing things about God with each other.

One day, Jamie told me about a disturbing note posted on one of the bulletin boards inside the dorm. The note alluded to exposing "spies who were reporting to the dean." Jamie told me she felt the author of the note was referring to us. I was really surprised.

"How can anyone think we are spies for the dean?" I asked her. Soon I noticed that people were avoiding us like the plague. People who normally walked with us to class no longer even spoke to us.

Then, one day Jamie directed me to another note on the board. It said that on a certain date at a certain time, the spies were going to be attacked. (This incident may sound crazy, but it really happened.) Jamie and I were scared. Her fears then turned to anger. During that time, we really sought the Lord for His protection.

To our surprise, an upper classman, whom all the girls respected, came out of her room at the very hour of the planned attack. She started screaming in the halls that if anyone wanted to fight, they would have to fight her. She didn't believe the false accusations and defended us. Guess what? From that day forward, not another word was spoken or written against us. People began to speak to us again.

Jamie and I were indeed dwelling in the secret place of the Most High. He delivered and protected us. I am very grateful knowing that God really is my refuge and fortress, my God in whom I trust.

Prayer

Lord, help me to remember that I need to dwell in Your secret place. Your abiding presence keeps me safe and secure. Help me to learn to trust You more and more. I thank You for all the security devices that have been created to protect us. I know that Your arms are more secure than any weapons made by man, so my trust is in Your power and ability. I acknowledge Your power, Lord, and I thank You for being my refuge and fortress, my God in whom I trust.

Evening

Fortress: Fortification, defender, defense, border.

He said: "The Lord is my rock, my fortress, and my deliverer."

(2 Sam. 22:2)

O my Strength, I watch for you; you, O God, are my fortress, my loving God.

(Ps. 59:9)

He alone is my rock and my salvation; he is my fortress, I will never be shaken.

(Ps. 62:2)

Most High: The highest God, the supreme God, Jehovah has judged, chief priest.

But Abram said to the king of Sodom, "I have raised my hand to the Lord, God Most High, Creator of heaven and earth, and have taken an oath."

(Gen. 14:22)

My shield is God Most High who saves the upright in heart.

(Ps. 7:10)

Psalm 91:1–2

____

____

____

Exercise

What have you been taught about trusting others? What has your experience been? In what ways have you felt abandoned by God in the past? Read Mark 15:34–16:7. In this account, Jesus felt abandoned by God. Did God actually abandon Jesus? If so, how? What victory came out of Jesus' experience on the cross? Write down your thoughts.

Journal Exercise

Promise: ______________________________

Principle: ______________________________

Application: ______________________________

DAY 15

His Truth

Morning

His truth shall be your shield and buckler.

(Ps. 91:4b NKJV)

My Shield and Buckler

Pontius Pilate asked Jesus, "What is truth?" Truth to one person is not truth to another person. We can twist truth until it becomes a confusing, chaotic, unreliable illusion. Yet there is only one truth—God's truth. After the dust settles and we stand before the Lord, we are measured by His truth, not ours. His truth is the only truth that matters. That is why it is our shield and buckler.

One of the first uses for the word shield referred to a stone for closing the entrance of a cave. Later shields referred to defensive devices made of various types of material such as leather, wood, or metal. They came in a variety of shapes to protect the whole person. A buckler was a smaller shield.

It was a common practice to go into battle with shields that had been oiled or anointed. Isaiah 21:5 makes mention of this practice. Oiling the shields helped to preserve them and made the enemies' missiles glide off more easily. We can think of God's truth as a preserver of life and a weapon that causes the attacks of the enemy to glide off.

History records that Pontius Pilate's truth resulted in torment for him. The Lord's truth, however, results in eternal salvation for those who embrace it.

Prayer

Lord, help me to see and apply Your truth in every situation. I acknowledge that I don't always see through an objective, perfect lens. My vision is sometimes distorted by my emotions, greed, selfishness, ambition, or past wounds. But, Lord, I know that Your precepts are right, and they give joy to my heart. I thank You for the availability of Your truth in my life, and I ask that Your shield and buckler not only surround me, but penetrate my innermost being.

Evening

Truth: Trustworthiness, fidelity, steadiness, reality, genuine, certainty; the manifested veritable essence of a matter.

> For your love is ever before me, and I walk continually in your truth.
>
> (Ps. 26:3)

> Into your hands I commit my spirit; redeem me, O Lord, the God of truth.
>
> (Ps. 31:5)

> Send forth your light and your truth, let them guide me; let them bring me to your holy mountain, to the place where you dwell.
>
> (Ps. 43:3)

Psalm 91:4b

____

____

"If you hold to my teaching, you are really my disciples. Then you will know the truth, and the truth will set you free."

(John 8:31b–32)

Exercise

How has the lens of your soul been distorted? How does applying God's truth help you to see the world more clearly?

Journal Exercise

Promise: ______________________________

Principle: ______________________________

Application: ______________________________

DAY 16

No Eternal Harm

Morning

> A thousand shall fall at your side and ten thousand at your right hand, but it shall not come near you.
>
> (Ps. 91:7)

Safe Throughout Eternity

Do you recall the story of the woman trapped under rubbage and debris after the terrorist attack on the World Trade Center in New York? You may recall another woman describing how she heard the Holy Spirit tell her to get out of the building when she was told to return to her desk after the first impact. These people acknowledged God throughout the horrible event.

We know that some believers did not survive the attack. How do we explain their loss? We can't, if we think of their lives as lost. But God tells us that to be absent from this body is to be present with the Lord. We can only lose our lives if we reject Him and hold on to the shallow things and philosophies of this world. If you are spared to live longer, or if you escape eternal death by being delivered into His salvation, it (the harm) does not come near you. Let's pray that masses would accept God's invitation for His eternal salvation.

Prayer

Father God, I thank You that because I am Yours, eternal harm has passed over me. You said that a thousand may fall at my side and ten thousand at my right hand, but it shall not come near me. In Your arms I am safe throughout eternity. Please help me to see Your protection in every situation, in every transition in my life. Lord, just as You are my eternal salvation, I pray now that others would come to know of Your great love and Your gracious invitation for eternal salvation.

Evening

Shield: The one who guards, wards off blows, and protects every part.

After this the word of the Lord came to Abram in a vision: "Do not be afraid, Abram, I am your shield, your very great reward."

(Gen. 15:1)

Blessed are you, O Israel! Who is like you, a people saved by the Lord? He is your shield and helper and your glorious sword.

(Deut. 33:29)

But you are a shield around me, O Lord; you bestow glory on me and lift up my head.

(Ps. 3:3)

The Lord is my strength and my shield; my heart trusts in him, and I am helped. My heart leaps for joy and I will give thanks to him in song.

(Ps. 28:7)

Psalm 91:7

____

____

____

____

Exercise

Write down what you learned about a shield from the previous day. Visualize yourself being surrounded by God the shield. How does it feel? Talk to God about shielding you. Journalize your thoughts.

Journal Exercise

Promise: ______________________________

Principle: ______________________________

Application: ______________________________

DAY 17

Sender of Angels

Morning

For He shall give His angels charge over you, to keep you in all your ways. In their hands they shall bear you up lest you dash your foot against a stone.

(Ps. 91:11–12 NKJV)

Our Other Helpers

I once heard a story about a missionary serving in another country. A group of hostile individuals threatened his life and were taking action to harm or kill him. His life was spared, and people came to Christ because of the incident. He later asked a man who had been part of the hostile group what stopped them. The man replied that when they saw very large men with weapons on the roof of the missionary's home, they got scared. Of course, the missionary did not know who the large men were. There was no other explanation for these strange helpers except that God sent His angels to help in time of trouble.

In my own life I have had some interesting experiences. Early one morning, as I was driving to work, when it was still dark, I saw a car coming right at me. I thought I was going to be hit. Incredibly, our cars did not collide. It was mind-boggling because it seemed that in the blink of an eye, the oncoming car shifted its course. I was very relieved and surprised that our cars did not collide. I immediately thought that God intervened in that situation. You can imagine how very grateful I am to God for watching over me. Let's not forget the powerful resources God provides when we call on Him for help.

Prayer

Father, how grateful I am for the angels that You have assigned over me. I ask that You dispatch Your angels to protect and minister on my behalf. Lord, it is such a privilege to have such powerful resources available to me. I thank You for the relationship and the covenant I have with You that enable angels to have charge over me. Thank You for sending me help in critical circumstances.

Evening

Protector: The one who shelters and covers.

Blessed is he who has regard for the weak; the Lord delivers him in times of trouble. The Lord will protect him and preserve his life; he will bless him in the land and not surrender him to the desires of his foes.

(Ps. 41:1–2)

Psalm 91:14

___

___

___

Sender of angels: The Most High God who dispatches spiritual helpers who serve in the capacity of messengers, warriors, and attendants to carry out His orders.

> Then Nebuchadnezzar said, Praise be to the God of Shadrach, Meshach and Abednego, who has sent his angel and rescued his servants. They trusted in him and defied the king's command and were willing to give up their lives rather than serve or worship any god except their own God.
>
> (Dan. 3:28)

> "My God sent his angel, and he shut the mouths of the lions. They have not hurt me, because I was found innocent in his sight. Nor have I ever done any wrong before you, O king."
>
> (Dan. 6:22)

> The Son of Man will send out his angels, and they will weed out of his kingdom everything that causes sin and all who do evil.
>
> (Matt. 13:41)

> Are not all angels ministering spirits sent to serve those who inherit salvation?
>
> (Heb. 1:14)

Exercise

What have you learned about angels in the above scriptures? Do you believe that God still uses angels today to minister protection to those who call out for help? What do the scriptures teach us about the attitudes of those who received help from God's ministering angels?

Journal Exercise

Promise: ______________________________

Principle: ______________________________

Application: ______________________________

DAY 18

The Lord God Almighty is with Me

Morning

> David then took up residence in the fortress and called it the City of David. He built up the area around it, from the supporting terraces inward. And he became more and more powerful, because the Lord God Almighty was with him.
>
> (2 Sam. 5:9–10)

Make God Your Foundation

Let's analyze what David did. He took up residence in the fortress of Zion. That means he lived in the fortified place of a major city. He planted himself inside a stronghold. Then he built up the area around it. Likewise, as we allow the Lord to take residence in us and plant our feet on His solid rock, we can then start building up our inner man with the Word of God through praise, meditation, and prayer. That is called abiding in Him. The Word of God is the foundation upon which we need to build our lives.

David became more powerful because the Lord God Almighty was with him. He spent time talking, writing, and singing to God, as well as meditating on God's Word. We also become more powerful as we read and meditate on His Word regularly. Why? Because the Word causes our faith to work in various situations. It becomes a voice that guides, strengthens, and leads us. We then can say, "The Lord God Almighty is with us."

Prayer

Father, I bid You to take up residence in me. Holy Spirit, guide my life and help me to build up myself with psalms, hymns, spiritual songs, and meditating on Your Word. Your Word, Lord, is a lamp unto my feet and a light unto my path. My trust is in Your Word, not my circumstances. Thank You for being my solid rock, my foundation. I praise You because You sustain me.

Evening

Almighty: Absolute sovereignty.

2 Samuel 5:9–10

____

____

____

____

____

____

The Spirit of God has made me; the breath of the Almighty gives me life.

(Job 33:4)

Hate evil, love good; maintain justice in the courts. Perhaps the Lord God Almighty will have mercy on the remnant of Joseph.

(Amos 5:15)

So, he said to me, "This is the word of the Lord to Zerubbabel; 'Not by might nor by power, but by my Spirit,' says the Lord Almighty."

(Zech. 4:6)

Look! The wages you failed to pay the workmen who mowed your fields are crying out against you. The cries of the harvesters have reached the ears of the Lord Almighty.

(James 5:4)

Each of the four living creatures had six wings and was covered with eyes all around, even under his wings. Day and night they never stop saying: "Holy, holy, holy is the Lord God Almighty, who was, and is, and is to come."

(Rev. 4:8)

Exercise

Write out three different scriptures containing the word Almighty. What do these Scriptures tell you about God? What do they tell you about man? How do you see the Lord Almighty working in your own life?

Journal Exercise

Promise: ______________________________

Principle: ______________________________

Application: ______________________________

DAY 19

God Avenges Me

Morning

And as they were drinking wine on that second day, the king asked again, "Queen Esther, what is your petition? It will be given you. What is your request? Even up to half the kingdom, it will be granted." Then Queen Esther answered, "If I have found favor with you, O king, and if it pleases your majesty, grant me my life—this is my petition. And spare my people—this is my request. For I and my people have been sold for destruction and slaughter and annihilation . . . King Xerxes asked Queen Esther, "Who is he? Where is the man who has dared [to presume in his heart] to do such a thing?"

(Esther 7:2–5)

He Will Save His People

Can you imagine the anger experienced by a loving Father toward those forces who would try to destroy His loved ones? God is not without emotion and passion. God is not intimidated by man. God is strong and He is with us. He is more real than we are. We may not understand His ways entirely, but we can depend on this: He will save His people.

The story of Esther ends with the king decreeing that God's people were not to be attacked. As a matter of fact, Haman, the one who perpetrated the plot to destroy God's people, was hanged on the very gallows he had constructed for Esther's uncle. The king also allowed God's people to defend themselves and destroy those who planned them harm. God cares for His covenanted people. It took the boldness of one woman who dared to call a nation to humble themselves with prayer and fasting that saved them. Just as Esther did, our calling out to Him will reap His victory in our lives.

Prayer

Father, I understand that life has its share of adversity, and sometimes we are faced with unwarranted attacks. Please help us as we go through times of uncertainty. People who possibly have never crossed our paths have planned for our destruction. Just as You helped Queen Esther and her people when plans were made against them for their destruction, I ask that You help us. Provide for us a safe haven and let us see deliverance with our own eyes.

Evening

Avenger: The one who redeems, punishes, or brings about vengeance.

He is the God who avenges me, who puts the nations under me . . .

(2 Sam. 22:48)

Esther 7:2–5

____

____

____

____

He is the God who avenges me, who subdues nations under me, who saves me from my enemies.

(Ps. 18:47–48a)

O Lord, the God who avenges, O God who avenges, shine forth.

(Ps. 94:1)

For the day of vengeance was in my heart, and the year of my redemption has come.

(Isa. 63:4)

> The Lord is a jealous and avenging God; the Lord takes vengeance and is filled with wrath. The Lord takes vengeance on his foes and maintains his wrath against his enemies.
>
> (Nah. 1:2)

Exercise

Why is God called an avenging God? What should your attitude be toward your enemies? Why is it important to hear from God regarding how to handle our enemies?

Journal Exercise

Promise:

Principle:

Application:

DAY 20

Who Can Stand Against God?

Morning

. . . Who then is able to stand against me? Who has a claim against me that I must pay? Everything under heaven belongs to me.

(Job 41:10b–11)

Possessor of Heaven and Earth

Some people think of God as distant and silent. One misperception they have is that an invisible God is not powerful, nor does He get involved in the lives of His people. We tend to put our faith in the physical realm, and we fail to see strength or power in the unseen. Even though we don't see God physically walking the earth, He is very much involved in the lives of those who call out to Him. As a matter of fact, God has been orchestrating and acting on behalf of His people before the foundation of the world. God, the possessor of heaven and earth, is very detailed and wise—so much so that He can devise a remedy to a problem before the problem manifests itself.

God knew before the world began that it would need to have Him eternally involved. He knew the heart of man. The world became filled with sin, sickness, and hopelessness. As a result, man needed someone who could save him from destruction. God knew Jesus

Christ (the Anointed One) was the solution for man's need for a Savior. The Bible tells us that Jesus, the Lamb of God, was slain before the world began. The Bible also tells us that Jesus forever makes intercession for us. That means we are so special to Him that He prays on our behalf to the Father.

In addition to what God has already provided for man, He has given us another solution to our needs. As we pray (according to His Word) in Jesus' Name, that prayer becomes the key that unlocks the door to the Father's heart. Out of the heart of our Father God flows the very thing we need for any situation.

God is the Omnipotent Father. He created the heavens and earth by taking order out of chaos. He took an incarcerated servant and made him the second most powerful man in Egypt. He delivered the Israelites out of slavery, and He sent a Savior to a dying world. No person, weapon, or nation can stand against Him. How then can a created being shun the Person who created him? How can we rail against the One to whom everything under heaven belongs?

Prayer

Father, I thank You that You are omnipotent, full of power and strength. Who are we to rail against One as powerful as You? We cannot truly understand Your infinity, nor do we truly understand Your limitless power. Your ways are higher than our ways, and Your thoughts higher than our thoughts. Forgive us for our lofty and haughty ways. We are grateful we can call You Father, our Maker, our Lord, our Savior. You truly reign over the heavens and the earth. No source or power can destroy You. We are protected under Your wings.

Evening

Possessor: The one who creates, procures; the landowner; the keeper.

God blessed them and said to them, "Be fruitful and increase in number; fill the earth and subdue it. Rule over the fish of the sea and the birds of the air and over every living creature that moves on the ground."

(Gen 1:28)

> And he blessed him and said, Blessed be Abram by God Most High, Possessor and Maker of heaven and earth.
>
> (Gen 14:19 AMP)

> The whole land of Canaan, where you are now an alien, I will give as an everlasting possession to you and your descendants after you; and I will be their God.
>
> (Gen. 17:8)

> Understand, then, that it is not because of your righteousness that the Lord your God is giving you this good land to possess, for you are a stiff-necked people.
>
> (Deut. 9:6)

Job 41:10b–11

____

____

____

> He made him master of his household, ruler over all he possessed.
>
> (Ps. 105:21)

Exercise

How does God as possessor of heaven and earth affect our needs and desires? In addition to possessor, what other attributes of God do you see from the morning's scripture? Explain.

Journal Exercise

Promise:

Principle:

Application:

DAY 21

Earthly Wisdom

Morning

> The wise will be put to shame; they will be dismayed and trapped. Since they have rejected the word of the Lord, what kind of wisdom do they have?
>
> (Jer. 8:9)

The Pig Bones Judgment

One of my first jobs as an adult was with a large oil company. One day the company received very disturbing news. Inside a burned company truck, police found the remains of some bones. Initially they thought the bones belonged to the driver of the truck. It turned out that the bones found inside the truck belonged to a pig. There was no sign of the driver anywhere. Authorities suspected foul play. After some time elapsed, the driver was found. He had planned to benefit financially from his staged death. Indeed, he did not benefit from his plans. The driver's earthly wisdom placed him before a judge who determined his fate.

Sometimes we need to assess whether the wisdom we depend on is based on our own intellect and emotions, or whether it is based on the wisdom of God's Word. Our intellect is not a bad thing because God gave it to us. When we chose to exploit and pervert that intellect, it becomes dangerous to our souls. Rejecting God's wisdom and replacing it with our own wisdom results in our ultimate shame. God said that person will be trapped. A trap is something that catches a person off guard. It is unexpected. Things may be rosy for a while, but one day, the trap will entangle that person and put him to shame. Trust in the wisdom of God.

Prayer

Father, search me to see what kind of wisdom I am operating from. I realize I don't always rely on Your wisdom. When I stray from Your wisdom, please nudge me, talk to me, push me, or do whatever it takes to have me hear and receive Your wisdom. Your wisdom produces life and gives me favor. My life is simply a mess without Your intervention. I don't want to be put to shame before You. I want to please You. Please help me, Lord.

Evening

Judge: Advocate, decide, try, convict, interrogate, determine, rule.

May the God of Abraham and the God of Nahor, the God of their father, judge between us.

(Gen. 31:53)

Those who oppose the Lord will be shattered. He will thunder against them from heaven; the Lord will judge the ends of the earth.

(1 Sam. 2:10)

He will judge the world in righteousness; he will govern the peoples with justice.

(Ps. 9:8)

Jeremiah 8:9

____

____

____

____

Exercise

How has your earthly wisdom gotten you into trouble in the past? Do you see a pattern in your own life that has caused problems for you? What can you do to change that? Ask God to show you how you can make your life more productive. How can you implement the information He gives you?

Journal Exercise

Promise: ____________________

Principle: ____________________

Application: ____________________

DAY 22

Witness About God's Goodness

Morning

You will be his witness to all men of what you have seen and heard. And now what are you waiting for? Get up, be baptized, and wash your sins away, calling on his name.

(Acts 22:15–16)

Healing of Painful Memories

"When the light from the policeman's flashlight shined upon the hard concrete, I saw masses of water bugs that had been crushed by the weight of two bodies—my attacker's and mine. It was a very shameful experience. It was a few months past my thirteenth birthday."

As Doreen shared this story with one of the women entering the rehabilitation program, she sat in disbelief. "You look like you never had any problems!" the woman exclaimed. "You just seem to have had the perfect life."

"I can assure you," Doreen told her, "much of my life was filled with pain and disappointment. At times I wanted to end my life. What you see today is a product of allowing

Jesus to heal me of many painful memories. And, there's still more work for Him to do." Doreen smiled and assured her that God could do the same for her. "Would you like to receive Christ as your personal Savior?" she asked.

"Yes," the woman said with tears in her eyes.

Though the experience was painful for a young girl to deal with, looking back, Doreen was able to see God's protection and provision. The gun the attacker had pointed at Doreen's side didn't go off; also, for some reason, he suddenly released his hold on her and ran.

God wants us to proclaim His truth and to testify of Him to others. The time is ripe to get right with God and to tell others about His love, healing, and delivering power. If you don't know how to get right with God, simply do what He says. Call on Him. Tell Him what's on your heart. Talk to Him as if you are talking with a trusted friend or counselor—for that is what He is.

Prayer

Father, I need You. I confess my sins of ______________ against You and others. I know that I sometimes blame You for my problems. I have also rejected You in the past because of hurts and disappointments. Please forgive me and set me on a straight path. I believe that Jesus is the way, the truth, and the life. I don't want to reject You any longer. I want You to be a major part of my life. I ask that Jesus would come into my life and put me on a right path.

Evening

Baptizer: The initiator of the Christian experience; the administrator of baptism. Baptism with the Holy Spirit anoints and energizes a believer for special service.

> I will pour out my Spirit on all people. Your sons and daughters will prophesy, your old men will dream dreams, your young men will see visions.
>
> (Joel 2:28)

I baptize you with water for repentance. But after me will come one who is more powerful than I, whose sandals I am not fit to carry. He will baptize you with the Holy Spirit and with fire.

(Matt. 3:11)

Acts 22:15–16

Or don't you know that all of us who were baptized into Christ Jesus were baptized into his death? We were therefore buried with him through baptism into death in order that, just as Christ was raised from the dead through the glory of the Father, we too may live a new life.

(Rom. 6:3–4)

And this water symbolizes baptism that now saves you also—not the removal of dirt from the body but the pledge of a good conscience toward God. It saves you by the resurrection of Jesus Christ, who has gone into heaven and is at God's right hand—with angels, authorities and powers in submission to him.

(1 Pet. 3:21–22)

Exercise

Who is the baptizer? What does baptism symbolize? How does being baptized relate to your witnessing about what God has done for you?

Journal Exercise

Promise:

Principle:

Application:

DAY 23

I Want to Know Christ

MORNING

But whatever was to my profit, I now consider loss for the sake of Christ. What is more, I consider them rubbish that I may gain Christ and be found in him, not having a righteousness of my own that comes from the law, but that which is through faith in Christ—the righteousness that comes from God and is by faith. I want to know Christ and the power of his resurrection and the fellowship of sharing his sufferings, becoming like him in his death, and so, somehow, to attain to the resurrection from the dead.

(Phil. 3:7–11)

The Rewards of Following Christ

Why do we feel that it is so hard to follow Christ? He even told us that His yoke is easy and His burdens are light. Some people believe that following Christ means living a mundane life devoid of good times. We seem to think that following Him means giving up our dreams and living a life of drudgery. Why would God tell us that He wants us to have life more abundantly if it were not so?

Many of the desires and passions we have are given to us from the Lord. He has bestowed gifts in each of us in order that we live an abundant life that glorifies Him. And what's so wrong with glorifying the Creator? After all, He's given us all things freely. So what are we really giving up? You will find that living a life for Him is far more profitable than you think. Those passionate longings we have to achieve and do something worthy in this lifetime were built into us from birth. We sometimes bury them because we think they are unachievable. But give them over to Him. Lose them in Him and see what He does with them. He will help us to birth those dreams.

Paul, who wrote the highlighted scripture (Phi. 3:7–11), was a brilliant man. When Christ approached him about his destiny, he immediately followed and willingly gave up his position, his philosophies—his all. But he found out that he had lost nothing, because a greater reward awaited Him. Before that, he was passionate about attacking Christ. He then became passionate about proclaiming the truth about Christ. It turned out that Paul contributed more to the New Testament than any other person. Indeed, he lost nothing and he had no regrets. We also will have no regrets when we turn our life and our passions over to the Lord.

Prayer

Lord, help me to lose myself in You. Help me to truly understand all that I have in You. I want to know You and the power of Your resurrection and the fellowship of Your suffering. Help me to know how much You care about my deepest longings. Help me to see that in following You, my life will be much richer than ever. Let me live the life You choose for me to live. I thank You for showing me how.

Evening

Righteous servant/Suffering servant: Holy servant; the one who makes right; the Savior who endured affliction and hardship with patience.

> After the suffering of his soul, he will see the light of life, and be satisfied; by his knowledge my righteous servant will justify many, and he will bear their iniquities. Therefore I will give him a portion among the great, and he will divide the spoils with the strong, because he poured out his life unto death, and was numbered with the transgressors, for he bore the sin of many, and made intercession for the transgressors.
>
> (Isa. 53:11–12)

Philippians 3:7–11

Exercise

Why did God accept the suffering of Jesus to make atonement for our sins? How has His suffering impacted your life? Read through Leviticus 1 to find out how man approached God before Jesus' sacrifice. According to Hebrews 4:16, how should you approach God? Journalize your thoughts regarding Jesus' sacrifice.

Journal Exercise

Promise:

Principle:

Application:

DAY 24

Don't Worry About Evil Men

Morning

Do not fret because of evil men or be envious of those who do wrong; for like grass they will soon wither, like green plants they will soon die away . . . I have seen a wicked and ruthless man flourishing like a green tree in its native soil, but he soon passed away and was no more; though I looked for him, he could not be found.

(Ps. 37:1–2; 35–36)

The Trappings of Wicked Living

God wants us not to make the mistake of thinking that evil men always win. They don't. They don't ever win. They will end up tangling themselves in a web of manipulation and dishonesty that will eventually backfire. They will also ultimately face the consequences of their actions before a holy and righteous God. The story of Ahab and Jezebel gives us a very clear picture of two powerful people who refused to amend their ways. After numerous warnings to change, they eventually destroyed themselves (1 Kings 16–22). The Bible promises that those who are just and righteous will be helped and protected by God for all eternity. Embracing the good pays off in this life and in the next.

Prayer

Father, help me to see that those who are evil really don't win in the end despite what I hear and see around me. Hurting others has no reward except negative consequences. Please, Father, lead me not into temptation but deliver me from evil. I have Your promise that if I live an upright life after Your ways, I have Your protection throughout all eternity. I choose to embrace the good. Help me to work out my salvation with fear and trembling so that I may please You.

EVENING

Righteous/Just: The holy one who is straight, makes right, safe, equitable, and provides proper judgment.

Psalm 37:1–2, 35–36

From the ends of the earth we hear singing: "Glory to the Righteous One."

(Isa. 24:16)

You are always righteous, O Lord, when I bring a case before you. Yet I would speak with you about your justice: Why does the way of the wicked prosper? Why do all the faithless live at ease?

(Jer. 12:1)

The Lord did not hesitate to bring the disaster upon us, for the Lord our God is righteous in everything he does; yet we have not obeyed him.

(Dan. 9:14)

God is just: He will pay back trouble to those who trouble you and give relief to you who are troubled, and to us as well. This will happen when the Lord Jesus is revealed from heaven in blazing fire with his powerful angels.

(2 Thess. 1:6–7)

Exercise

What does God remind man concerning the wicked? What reward do the wicked receive for their deeds? What are your thoughts concerning the wicked? Have you allowed those thoughts to affect your perception of living a righteous life?

Journal Exercise

Promise: ____

Principle: ____

Application: ____

DAY 25

Don't Be Troubled—God Has a Special Promise for You

Morning

Do not let your hearts be troubled. Trust in God; trust also in me. In my Father's house are many rooms; if it were not so, I would have told you. I am going there to prepare a place for you.

(John 14:1–2)

A Special Place for Me

"Now what style are you looking for, ma'am?" he asked.

"I'm not sure. I like the English Tudor. Yet I like the Victorian style, and I also like a rancher," she replied.

"Come with me," he said. "I know just what you want." He led her into his office and pointed to a large book on his desk. "Open the book to page 307," he directed. "Is this what you have in mind?" he asked.

"My goodness!" she exclaimed. "I can't believe you know exactly what I want."

It's a heartwarming and exciting thought to know that Jesus went ahead of us to prepare a special place for us. An exciting future awaits us. Even though the world may appear to be crazy and out-of-control, we can look forward to a stable, secure place prepared just for us. It will suit every need and desire within our hearts. Let's rejoice for the beautiful eternity prepared just for us.

Prayer

Father, I want to praise and thank You for preparing a special place just for me. How can I thank You enough for all You've done and all You have planned for me? You are a merciful, kind, and loving God, and You always deserve my highest praise. Surely, there is none like You. I love You.

Evening

Father of promise/Father of divine promise: Paternal assertion and self-committal, the Word; the One who is responsible for the care and nurturing of His children.

> O Sovereign Lord, you are God! Your words are trustworthy, and you have promised these good things to your servant.
>
> (2 Sam. 7:28)

> For he remembered his holy promise given to his servant Abraham.
>
> (Ps. 105:42)

> The days are coming, declares the Lord, when I will fulfill the gracious promise I made to the house of Israel and to the house of Judah.
>
> (Jer. 33:14)

John 14:1–2

> By faith Abraham, even though he was past age—and Sarah herself was barren—was enabled to become a father because he considered him faithful who had made the promise.
>
> (Heb. 11:11)

Exercise

Why does God tell us not to worry? What has God promised us? How can you prepare yourself for what He has promised? What activated the promises of God in Abraham's life? What can you do to activate the promises of God in your life?

Journal Exercise

Promise: ______________________________

Principle: ______________________________

Application: ______________________________

DAY 26

You Have a Personal Counselor

Morning

And I will ask the Father, and he will give you another Counselor to be with you forever—the Spirit of truth . . .

(John 14:16–17a)

A Valuable Friend

How often do we not recognize or take advantage of the wonderful Friend who is available to us in the person of the Holy Spirit? The Holy Spirit is an invaluable gift who is able to speak with us throughout the day. The little nudges we sometimes experience for daily decisions; a verse that sticks out above all others during our devotional time; a friend saying just the right thing at the right time; the minister teaching about the very situation that we are going through; the peaceful, comforting presence at critical moments. What a powerful Friend. Let's take a moment to thank Him for the valuable and loving Friend that He is. He is our holy treasure.

Prayer

Father, I thank You for the gift of the Holy Spirit. It was Your wisdom and Your love that required such a beautiful gift be intimately involved in our lives. I recognize the Holy

Spirit's beautiful yet powerful awesomeness. I am grateful that He leads and guides and counsels me. I am grateful that He comforts me. He is truly more precious than silver and more costly than gold. He's my advocate, my advisor, and my paraclete, for He walks beside me. This gift from You, Lord, I treasure.

Evening

Paraclete/Counselor: The one called to another's side to help, console, exhort/supporter; advisor; leader.

John 14:16–17a

But the Counselor, the Holy Spirit, whom the Father will send in my name, will teach you all things and will remind you of everything I have said to you.

(John 14:26)

But I tell you the truth: It is good that I am going away. Unless I go away, the Counselor will not come to you; but if I go, I will send him to you. When he comes, he will convict the world of guilt in regard to sin and righteousness and judgment: in regard to sin, because men do not believe in me; in regard to righteousness, because I am going to the Father, where you can see me no longer; and in regard to judgment, because the prince of this world now stands condemned.

(John 16:7–11)

Intercessor: The one who makes petition to the Father on behalf of another.

In the same way, the Spirit helps us in our weakness. We do not know what we ought to pray for, but the Spirit himself intercedes for us with groans that words cannot express. And he who searches our hearts knows the mind of the Spirit, because the Spirit intercedes for the saints in accordance with God's will.

(Rom. 8:26–27)

Exercise

What is the significance of the Holy Spirit in our lives? Look through the Book of Acts and find an incident where the Holy Spirit provides direction. Write down what you've learned. Based on what you have read so far about the Holy Spirit, why do we say that He is a person? How should you respond to the Holy Spirit?

Journal Exercise

Promise: ____________________

Principle: ____________________

Application: ____________________

DAY 27

My Help

Morning

> I will lift up my eyes to the hills—from whence comes my help? My help comes from the Lord, who made heaven and earth.
>
> (Ps. 121:1–2 NKJV)

Lift Up Your Eyes

Have you ever noticed what happens when you lift up your eyes? Looking up puts your mind in a position of hopefulness, expectancy, and optimism. The meditation within your heart transitions from a negative to a positive state. When you begin to meditate on the God who made heaven and earth, not only does your whole view change, but your vision changes as well.

Notice what happens when you are depressed and unsettled. You look down and everything becomes dismal, bleak, and negative. God, our Creator, who put together the intricacies of the universe, can surely piece together and resolve any problem you may encounter. On top of that, He gives you a new vision and a fresh start. It can't get any better than that.

Prayer

God, I thank You that You, the Creator of heaven and earth, are able to put my life back together. I am so grateful for Your involvement in my life. I know there is no problem You cannot resolve. Lord, I lift up my eyes to You and thank You for Your help and new vision.

Evening

Creator of the ends of the earth/You who dwell in the heavens: The one who fashioned the earth; founder of the earth/the one whose presence fills the heavens.

Psalm 121:1–2

____

____

____

____

I lift up my eyes to you, to you whose throne is in heaven.

(Ps. 123:1)

Do you not know? Have you not heard? The Lord is the everlasting God, the Creator of the ends of the earth. He will not grow tired or weary and his understanding no one can fathom.

(Isa. 40:28)

. . . He who made the Pleiades and Orion, who turns blackness into dawn and darkens day into night, who calls for the waters of the sea and pours them out over the face of the land—the Lord is his name—he flashes destruction on the stronghold and brings the fortified city to ruin.

(Amos 5:8–9)

Exercise

Why is it important to understand who made the heavens and the earth? How does this understanding affect your view of God's abilities? When trouble comes your way, which view do you focus on and where do you look? What can you do to keep your focus on God?

Journal Exercise

Promise: ______________________________

Principle: ______________________________

Application: ______________________________

DAY 28

The Incomparable God

Morning

"To whom will you compare me? Or who is my equal?" says the Holy One. Lift your eyes and look to the heavens! Who created all these? He who brings out the starry host one by one, and calls them each by name. Because of his great power and mighty strength, not one of them is missing.

(Isa. 40:25–26)

The Wisdom of Our Creator

"The sun is located in a galaxy called what?" Mrs. Henkle asked her class.

"The Milky Way!" they said in unison.

"Good," she said. "And how many stars does the Milky Way galaxy contain?"

"Mrs. Henkle, I know. I know!" shouted Beverly.

"So do I, Mrs. Henkle," said Crystal.

"Okay," she responded. "Both of you ladies write the answer on the board."

They walked excitedly to the blackboard and wrote their numbers.

"Ronald, do you agree with what they wrote?" Mrs. Henkle asked.

"Well," Ronald stammered. "Can I look at my notes from yesterday?" he asked.

"Take a guess, Ronald."

"Okay, Mrs. Henkle, it's . . ."

Before he could get the number out, his twin brother, Donald, blurted out, "One hundred billion stars, Mrs. Henkle."

"Now, Donald," she said, "you should have given your brother the opportunity to answer my question."

"Mrs. Henkle, I know scientists believe there are more than 100 billion galaxies in the universe," Ronald stated.

"That's very good, Ronald. Girls, thank you. You did a great job," she said, dismissing them from the blackboard.

Our Creator taught man much about His creation. The Book of Job mentions that God is the Maker of the "Bear, Orion, the Pleiades and the constellations of the south" (Job 9:9). It's very interesting indeed, especially since Job is considered to be one of the oldest poetic books in the Bible.

Not only does God teach about the universe, He also teaches about human health. His dietary laws promoted optimum health for the Israelites. They are still followed today by many people. His proverb stating the importance of laughter has been confirmed by recent studies. Proverb 17:22 says, "A cheerful heart is good medicine, but a crushed spirit dries up the bones." Think about it. Scientists have discovered that laughter releases a hormone that promotes healing. We know that a damaged, crushed spirit brings about various types of emotional and physical problems. How then can we have uncertainties about the wisdom of the Creator? He is without a doubt the incomparable One to call on for help, protection, and direction.

Prayer

Holy Father, help me to see how big You really are. I know that I can always be secure knowing that Your eyes watch over me. You created the galaxies containing all the starry hosts. You're the Creator of the ends of the earth. I thank You for knowing and caring for me.

Evening

Holy One: Sanctuary of deity; godly, sacred, clean, pure, consecrated.

The Lord Almighty is the one you are to regard as holy, he is the one you are to fear, he is the one you are to dread, and he will be a sanctuary.

(Isa. 8:13–14a)

Isaiah 40:25–26

This is what the Lord says—your Redeemer, the Holy One of Israel: I am the Lord your God, who teaches you what is best for you, who directs you in the way you should go.

(Isa. 48:17)

But just as he who called you is holy, so be holy in all you do; for it is written: "Be holy, because I am holy."

(1 Pet. 1:15–16)

Hallowed: Holy, sacred.

This then, is how you should pray: "Our Father in heaven, hallowed be your name, your kingdom come, your will be done on earth as it is in heaven."

(Matt. 6:9–10)

Exercise

Why is it important to know that God is holy? How can a holy God teach us about life? In view of God's holiness, how should you respond to Him? How should you respond to others? What changes can you make in your own life to respond to others as God desires and requires?

Journal Exercise

Promise:

Principle:

Application:

DAY 29

God Does Not Grow Tired

Morning

> Do you not know? Have you not heard? The Lord is the everlasting God, the Creator of the ends of the earth. He will not grow tired or weary, and his understanding no one can fathom.
>
> (Isa. 40:28)

Are You Tired?

She did not know how to tell her parents, but she knew that if they found out from another source, they would be devastated.

"Mom, Dad, can we talk?" Sally asked.

"What is it, honey?" her mom asked. "You sound very serious."

"I don't know how to tell you this, but . . ."

"But what?" her father asked in a demanding tone. "You're not pregnant, are you?"

"No, Dad, it's nothing like that," Sally responded. "I know how much both of you want me to be a doctor and how much money you've paid already for my schooling. It's just that I'm bored with school. I can't seem to get into it. I'm just tired of everything," she blurted out.

"But we thought this was what you wanted," her mom said with concern.

"Mom, I can't explain it. I thought I did, but the work is so hard. I am so tired," said Sally.

"Baby, let your mom and me take you out to dinner. You just need to relax a bit. Give yourself some time to think it over," her father said as he hugged her.

"But Dad . . . ," Sally responded.

"Well now, let's talk about your choices. Would taking a sabbatical help you? Come on, sweetheart," he said to his wife. "Let's call that Italian restaurant and make reservations for dinner."

Many times, we get tired of the different responsibilities we encounter. We want to take the easy way out and quit. Sometimes it just feels good not to have anything pulling at us, and we just want to chill out from life. Wouldn't it be awful if God chilled out on us? We would be in such pitiful shape. Because God doesn't grow tired or weary, we know He will fulfill His commitment to help us. He won't quit on us. He doesn't have a body that breaks down, and He knows just how to take care of us. He doesn't have to ask anyone for advice. He has perfect love and wisdom.

Prayer

Lord, You are beyond understanding. I am grateful that someone as omnipotent and loving as You would care for me every minute of the day. I am glad that when I grow tired, You don't. I am grateful that when I am weak, You are strong. You are the God who holds me up and carries me. Thank You for being patient with me. Thank You for Your strength.

Evening

Ancient of Days: The one who has unending existence; majestic, powerful, providential God.

> As I watched, this horn was waging war against the saints and defeating them, until the Ancient of Days came and pronounced judgment in favor of the saints of the Most High, and the time came when they possessed the kingdom.
>
> (Dan. 7:21–22)

Immortal: The one who lives forever; the one who does not decay; the one who existed before time began.

Isaiah 40:28

____

____

____

Now to the King eternal, immortal, invisible, the only God, be honor and glory forever and ever.

(1 Tim. 1:17)

King forever and ever: Sovereign throughout eternity.

For to us a child is born, to us a son is given, and the government will be on his shoulders. And he will be called Wonderful Counselor, Mighty God, Everlasting Father, Prince of Peace. Of the increase of his government and peace there will be no end. He will reign on David's throne and over his kingdom establishing and upholding it with justice and righteousness from that time on and forever. The zeal of the Lord will accomplish this.

(Isa. 9:6–7)

Exercise

What does God's sovereignty and immortality mean to you? How does that affect what you set as priorities in your life? What priorities have you set for your life? Would those priorities result in productive, fruitful living, or would they drain you and become burdensome? How can you know those priorities are line with God's purposes for your life?

Journal Exercise

Promise:

Principle:

Application:

DAY 30

The Lord Does Not Sleep

MORNING

He will not allow your foot to be moved; He who keeps you will not slumber. Behold, He who keeps Israel shall neither slumber nor sleep . . . The Lord shall preserve you from all evil; He shall preserve your soul.

(Ps. 121:3–4, 7 NKJV)

The Grateful

"Wake up, Sam," she said. "You will miss the inauguration."

"Sydney," said Sam lazily. "I don't want to go anywhere."

"But, Sam, he's our uncle."

"Sydney, will you lay off! I am not interested in anything he has to say," Sam snarled.

"He's done so much for us after our parents died. He took care of us. How can you be so nonchalant about attending his inauguration?" Sydney asked.

"He only did what he was supposed to do," Sam snapped.

"You ungrateful, spoiled brat!" she retorted as she left the room.

Two months later Sydney and Sam sat in the office of their uncle's attorney.

"I am sorry we had to meet under these circumstances," the attorney said.

"Well, yeah, get to the point," Sam said coldly.

"Mr. Derner instructed that his business be turned over to Sydney on the condition that you, Sam, would never be hired as an employee, business partner, consultant, or have any other connection with the firm. Your allowance will be cut off in six months. That should give you enough time to find suitable employment for yourself. Mr. Derner felt that Sydney invested time and money into learning the business and that she could be trusted with it," said the attorney.

"What?" Sam screamed.

"Don't you think fifteen years past your eighteenth birthday is ample time to have become responsible?" the attorney asked flatly. "That concludes your portion, Sam. There are more details I need to go over with you, Sydney," the attorney said, looking at her.

While everyone else is sleeping, God is not. That means He is working around the clock for those of us who belong to Him, to see that our needs are met and our lives are protected. He is the all-seeing, all-knowing God who has a resplendent empire of heavenly beings ready, willing, and able to give us help when we need it. Even while we are unaware of it, God preserves our souls. There is no need to fear about the future or anything that should afflict us because we have a God who is protective, loving, watchful, and wise.

Prayer

Lord, I am so grateful that You neither slumber nor sleep. You watch over me and preserve my soul. I don't ever have to worry about my life. I can sleep peacefully and comfortably knowing You are there with me. Thank You, Lord. Help me to know this truth in a much deeper way.

Evening

Preserver: The one who refreshes, guards, gives life to, saves, makes safe, and protects.

> In a dream, in a vision of the night, when deep sleep falls on men as they slumber in their beds, he may speak in their ears and terrify them with warnings, to turn man

from wrongdoing and keep him from pride, to preserve his soul from the pit, his life from perishing by the sword.

(Job 33:15–18)

The Lord will protect him and preserve his life; he will bless him in the land and not surrender him to the desire of his foes.

(Ps. 41:2)

Psalm 121:3–4, 7

___

___

___

___

Though I walk in the midst of trouble, you preserve my life; you stretch out your hand against the anger of my foes, with your right hand you save me.

(Ps. 138:7)

Exercise

In what ways has God preserved your life? How has your response been toward God? Write down three affirmations describing how God preserves your life.

Journal Exercise

Promise: ______________________________

Principle: ______________________________

Application: ______________________________

DAY 31

We Are Not Destroyed

Morning

> We are hard pressed on every side, yet not crushed. We are perplexed, but not in despair; persecuted, but not forsaken; struck down, but not destroyed—always carrying about in the body the dying of the Lord Jesus, that the life of Jesus also may be manifested in our body.
>
> (2 Cor. 4:8–10)

The Power In Us

Nothing, absolutely nothing, can destroy us if we are His. Why? Because the same Spirit that raised Jesus lives in us. There is a great power within us to withstand the hardships of life. That power is working in us whether we feel it or not. When we suffer, God uses that womb of pain as an incubator to produce greatness in us. It is up to us to use the suffering as an impetus to manifest that greatness. We must remember that Christ paid a huge price by suffering for our sake. Through His suffering, we reap the benefits. A simple prayer, a simple acknowledgement, a simple hope in God releases tremendous deliverance in our lives that only God can provide. In this release, storms are quieted, the winds cease, and fires abate.

Prayer

Lord, I am grateful for Your powerful deliverance. Because of You, and You only, I am neither crushed, in despair, forsaken, nor destroyed. I count it an honor to have the life of Jesus manifested in my body. Thank You for such tremendous deliverance.

Evening

Atoning sacrifice: The one who made Himself a tribute and offering to restore others to their proper positions. The one who became a covering. The expiator.

> After the suffering of his soul, he will see the light of life and be satisfied; by his knowledge my righteous servant will justify many, and he will bear their iniquities. Therefore I will give him a portion among the great, and he will divide the spoils with the strong, because he poured out his life unto death, and was numbered with the transgressors, for he bore the sin of many, and made intercession for the transgressors.
>
> (Isa. 53:11–12)

> He told them, "This is what is written: The Christ will suffer and rise from the dead on the third day, and repentance and forgiveness of sins will be preached in his name to all nations, beginning at Jerusalem."
>
> (Luke 24:46–47)

2 Corinthians 4:8–10

____

____

____

____

And by that will, we have been made holy through the sacrifice of the body of Jesus Christ once for all.

(Heb. 10:10)

Exercise

Jesus' life is an example of great suffering and sacrifice for the salvation of mankind. How did the apostle Paul relate to the sufferings of Christ (see 2 Cor. 4:8–10)? How do you relate to the sufferings of Christ? In what ways has Christ's suffering impacted you?

Journal Exercise

Promise: ____________________

Principle: ____________________

Application: ____________________

DAY 32

Nothing Can Separate Us From God's Love

MORNING

For I am persuaded that neither death nor life, nor angels nor principalities nor powers, nor things present nor things to come, nor height, nor depth, nor any other created thing shall be able to separate us from the love of God which is in Christ Jesus our Lord.

(Rom. 8:38–39 NKJV)

I Will Always Love You

She ran through the house nervously. "They found him. They found him!" she screamed. She had already informed her husband, and he was heading home to meet the police officers. She went into her son's room to make sure everything was in order.

I can't think, I am so nervous, she said to herself.

"Marcy," she said over the phone. "They found Tim. They found Tim!"

"I'll be right over," she said.

Fifteen minutes later, there was a knock on her door.

"Mrs. Greennuckle," the officer said, "here he is, safe and sound."

Tim appeared both frightened and relieved to be home.

"Mom, I'm sorry," he said.

She reached toward him and cried aloud.

"I was so worried. Don't ever do that to us again," she said.

"I was so angry. I just wanted to run away and never come back," Tim said sheepishly.

"But we thought you were dead. It's been four months," she said.

"Mrs. Greennuckle," the officer interrupted, "what was it you told me you wanted to say to your son if you ever saw him again?"

"Honey," she turned to Tim. "I love you. I will always love you. There is nothing you could ever do or say that will stop me from loving you." For the first time in ten years, she saw Tim cry.

This mother was so overjoyed to see her lost son return home. It did not matter what he did, she just wanted him back safe. Nothing could make her stop loving him. How much greater is God's love for us. His love for us is unfailing and never ending. Isn't it good to know that nothing or no one can separate us from His love? His love is what makes us feel safe and secure. His love is awesome.

Prayer

Thank You, Lord, that I am stuck to You like glue. I am stuck to You for life eternally, and nothing can cause Your love to be taken from those who love You and those who are in Christ Jesus. I will always love You. Your Word says that You will never leave me nor forsake me (Heb. 13:5). I can rest assured with the knowledge that You will never take Your love away from me. Thank You.

Evening

Shepherd and Overseer of my soul: The one who tends to and pastures a flock. The one who visits, cares for, and supervises.

> Hear us, O Shepherd of Israel, you who lead Joseph like a flock; you who sit enthroned between the cherubim, shine forth.
>
> (Ps. 80:1)

> For you were like sheep going astray, but now you have returned to the Shepherd and Overseer of your souls.
>
> (1 Pet. 2:25)

Lover of my soul: The promoter of virtue. The one who provides nurturing and affection for my soul.

> Jesus answered, "Everyone who drinks this water will be thirsty again, but whoever drinks the water I give him will never thirst. Indeed, the water I give him will become in him a spring of water welling up to eternal life."
>
> (John 4:13–14)

Romans 8:38–39

____

____

____

____

Exercise

Have you ever felt separated from God? What was going on in your life at that time? Were you trusting in God's Word concerning His unfailing love for you, or were you trusting in your emotions at the time? What happened that caused you to feel God's closeness again? Write down some biblical and personal examples of why you can trust God as the shepherd and lover of your soul.

Journal Exercise

Promise: ____________________

Principle: ____________________

Application: ____________________

DAY 33

No Weapon Can Hurt Me

Morning

"No weapon formed against you shall prosper, and every tongue which rises up against you in judgment you shall condemn. This is the heritage of the servants of the Lord, and their righteousness is from Me," says the Lord.

(Isa. 54:17 NKJV)

The Difficult Co-Worker

God does not hide the fact that we will be attacked. He tells us very clearly that weapons are formed against us. But He also gives us the assurance that attacks against us won't prosper. They won't stick.

I have a friend, Darlene, who started a new job. A younger woman wanted the position she was hired for. Darlene noticed that the woman made sarcastic remarks to her and was very difficult to deal with. The woman even tried to involve other co-workers in her complaints. Darlene kept the matter before the Lord. The managers and other co-workers soon realized that the young woman was purposefully making things difficult for Darlene.

One day, one of the managers confronted this young woman about her behavior. Afterwards, the young woman had a heart-to-heart talk with Darlene and apologized.

The final outcome of that situation was that Darlene embraced her like a spiritual daughter. God's Word is faithful. The weapon formed against Darlene did not prosper. Just as in Darlene's case, God wants us to stand still and see His deliverance.

Prayer

Lord, I thank You for Your honesty in letting me know that I am not excluded from attacks. Your Word gives me such confidence that the attacks won't destroy me. Because of my right standing with You, I can refute any wrong accusation against me and You will back me up. I will stand embraced by Your truth, peace, salvation, faith, and Word. I will stand still and see the deliverance of the Lord. Thank You for being there for me whenever I need You. You are truly my defense.

Evening

Defender: The one who protects, helps, delivers.

Isaiah 54:17

____

____

____

____

> Yet their Redeemer is strong; the Lord Almighty is his name. He will vigorously defend their cause so that he may bring rest to their land, but unrest to those who live in Babylon.
>
> (Jer. 50:34)

God of justice: The Spirit of formal decree; the life-giver that makes right.

> Yet the Lord longs to be gracious to you; he rises to show you compassion. For the Lord is a God of justice. Blessed are all who wait for him.
>
> (Isa. 30:18)

A sure foundation: My solid footing, base, and establishment.

> So this is what the Sovereign Lord says: "See, I lay a stone in Zion, a tested stone, a precious cornerstone for a sure foundation; the one who trusts will never be dismayed."
>
> (Isa. 28:16)

Exercise

What kind of foundation has God provided to ensure us of His devotion and care? Who can you trust when people perpetrate evil against you? Have you ever had someone accuse you falsely? What was the outcome? Did you put your trust in God to deliver you and avenge you of the wrong? How did you (or can you) release the matter into God's hands?

Journal Exercise

Promise: ______________________________

Principle: ______________________________

Application: ______________________________

DAY 34

God Comforts Me

Morning

As a father pities his children, so the Lord pities those who fear Him. For He knows our frame; He remembers that we are dust. As for man, his days are like grass; as a flower of the field, so he flourishes. For the wind passes over it, and it is gone, and its place remembers it no more. But the mercy of the Lord is from everlasting to everlasting on those who fear Him, and His righteousness to children's children, to such as keep His covenant, and to those who remember His commandments to do them. (Ps. 103:13–18 NKJV)

Comfort at the Right Moment

I had arrived in Maryland only two months before I received the shocking phone call. "Pam, Mom is gone," said my oldest sister Angie.

"What do you mean, gone?" I asked.

"I went upstairs to give her medication, and I couldn't wake her up."

It had been eighteen years since I lived in Maryland, and my family seemed very happy to have me back home. I had pretty much made California my home. God gave me wonderful friends who were like family, yet I felt God led me to move back home. I thought it would give me a good opportunity to bond with my mother. I had just lost my father two months before, and I knew I could be more of a help to my family if I moved back home.

The news of my mother's death, however, hit me quite hard. I was numb with grief. Here was a woman I hardly knew because she was a private, distant person in her relationship with most of her children; and there would not be any more opportunities to get to know her. I consoled myself in knowing she was at peace. She no longer had to worry about life without my father. She no longer had to worry about the many problems that plagued her.

As we walked toward the veterans' chapel for the final prayer before her body was laid to rest, I felt so alone. I looked around, and everyone seemed to be paired off. Two of my sisters had their children with them. Another sister had her husband. My daughter was walking with her husband.

"*Lord*," I said, "*I feel so alone. I don't have anyone*," I cried silently.

As soon as I finished speaking to Him, my daughter came up to me, hugged me, and kissed my cheek. I should not have been surprised. God knows what we need before we ask. How grateful I am to Him for providing me with comfort just at the right moment. What a compassionate Father He is.

Comfort from a loved one is enough to take away that awful feeling of failure, loneliness, and disappointment. We have a heavenly Father who pities our frail state and feeds us with His love and compassion. His love heals our heartache and disappointment. It is true; our heavenly Father makes everything all right.

Prayer

Heavenly Father, thank You for Your compassion toward me. I am so glad you are not harsh or insensitive. You truly are the Father of comfort. Your thoughts toward me are filled with love and for that, I am thankful. Let me be one of those who comforts others who are in need of comforting. Use me in this, I pray.

Evening

God of all comfort: The God who pities, consoles, refreshes, supports, encourages, and exhorts.

Psalm 103:13–18

Do not be afraid, for I am with you; I will bring your children from the east and gather you from the west.

(Isa. 43:5)

Praise be to the God and Father of our Lord Jesus Christ, the Father of compassion and the God of all comfort, who comforts us in all our troubles, so that we can comfort those in any trouble with the comfort we ourselves have received from God.

(2 Cor. 1:3–4)

Here is a trustworthy saying that deserves full acceptance: Christ Jesus came into the world to save sinners—of whom I am the worst. But for that very reason I was shown mercy so that in me, the worst of sinners, Christ Jesus might display his unlimited patience as an example for those who would believe on him and receive eternal life.

(1 Tim. 1:15–16)

Exercise

In what way does God make you feel loved and comforted? What does God want you to do in regard to others who need comfort? Can you think of any person who needs compassionate understanding and action? How can you help?

Journal Exercise

Promise: ______________________________

Principle: ______________________________

Application: ______________________________

DAY 35

God Does Not Condemn Me

Morning

There is therefore now no condemnation for those who are in Christ Jesus who walk not according to the flesh but according to the Spirit.

(Rom. 8:1 NKJV)

Moving Past Condemnation

When I arrived at the outreach center one morning and opened the back door, a group of people screamed, "Take her, take her! She needs a shower." I wasn't quite ready to open up the center, but there emerged a woman who reeked of indescribable odors. It was apparent she had not showered in days, maybe months. I could also see that she was delicate and emotionally unstable.

I led her to the shower and took out some fresh clothing for her. Instead of taking a shower, she insisted on bathing. After quite some time had elapsed, I managed to get her out of the bathroom. She really enjoyed the bath. During the time she was in the bathroom, I made conversation with her. It became obvious this woman experienced much abuse during her life. At one point, I told her, "God loves you, and so do I."

"I didn't know anyone could love a jailbird," she said with surprise in her voice.

Her words broke my heart. Here in my midst was a precious lady who thought no one could ever love her. I was so humbled and honored to have had the opportunity to serve her.

Much of our inability to move forward in life is due to guilt and feelings of worthlessness that we have inflicted upon ourselves. We also allow others to inflict those feelings upon us. If you examine the life of bitter, unforgiving, unstable, and fearful people, you may discover that somewhere in their lives, guilt and lack of self-worth began to direct their behavior. Though it is difficult for some of us to stop condemning ourselves, we need to take God at His Word that He's cool with us. He doesn't hate us for the wrongs we've done. Why else would He say, "As far as the east is from the west, so far have I removed your transgressions from you" (Ps. 103:12)?

If we are truly repentant for our wrongs, we must choose to move on with our lives, despite our consequences for the act and despite what others think or say. Just remember this truth—our eternal destination is not dependant upon what man thinks of us. It's dependant upon our relationship with God. Man has absolutely no say in the matter. God loves you. There's nothing you can do to make Him feel otherwise.

Prayer

Lord, here is another thing to be grateful for. I am grateful that You do not condemn me. I have been so blinded by guilt. It has impacted the way I perceive and treat others. Please forgive me for the act of ___________ and the effects the guilt has had upon me and others. Lord, I thank You that Your blood cleanses me, and You have removed my transgressions far from me. Heal me, Lord, and I will be healed.

Evening

Exonerator/God who forgives/God of all grace: The one who pardons/ God who covers, pardons/ God of beauty.

> For as high as the heavens are above the earth, so great is his love for those who fear him; as far as the east is from the west, so far has he removed our transgressions from us.
>
> (Ps. 103:11–12)

Romans 8:1

____

____

____

> And the God of all grace, who called you to his eternal glory in Christ, after you have suffered a little while, will himself restore you and make you strong, firm and steadfast.
>
> (1 Pet. 5:10)

Him who is able to present you faultless: The one who exonerates and pardons.

> To him who is able to keep you from falling and to present you before his glorious presence without fault and with great joy—to the only God our Savior be glory, majesty, power and authority, through Jesus Christ our Lord, before all ages, now and forevermore!
>
> (Jude 24–25)

Exercise

We are sometimes faced with two types of people: people who don't seem to feel remorse or sorry about hurting others and people who carry their guilt. What do you think are the underlying factors behind each type? Which category do you fall under?

If you are in the first category, ask God to soften and tenderize your heart, and to show you anything in your heart you need to be forgiven for. If you are in the second category, ask God to strengthen you and show you ways the enemy is using your guilt to keep you in bondage. In both cases, ask God for wisdom in your relationships with others. Write out how you will apply God's forgiveness in your own life.

Journal Exercise

Promise: ______________________________

Principle: ______________________________

Application: ______________________________

DAY 36

Forget the Past

MORNING

Brethren, I do not count myself to have apprehended; but one thing I do, forgetting those things which are behind, and reaching forward to those things which are ahead. I press toward the goal for the prize of the upward call of God in Christ Jesus.

(Phil. 3:13–14 NKJV)

The Gatekeeper

"Stop singing that!" she screamed to the gatekeeper. "Tell them to stop singing that!" she snarled.

"One day we will sing that for you, but you have to let go of certain things," said the gatekeeper.

"I won't let go of anything," the woman snarled. "I like my life. I am comfortable with it."

"It's your choice," responded the gatekeeper. "You can go to the next line. You can go to the next line. To the next line, to the next line, you can go. You can go." She heard the song over and over again. She was sick of it.

How can they expect me to forgive anyone? she thought. *The people in this place must be nuts!*

"Hey all you crazy people," she screamed, "shut up!"

Just then the gatekeeper appeared.

"You do know why they are singing, don't you?" the gatekeeper asked. "These people have chosen to release the hate and bitterness they felt toward those who have wronged them. There's now a beautiful, new experience waiting just for them. This is a big accomplishment for them."

"But you don't understand," the imprisoned woman wailed. "My uncle molested me. My husband cheated on me and left me. I was fired from my job!"

"Oh, but I do understand," the gatekeeper said. "I understand all too well. My uncle molested me. My husband cheated on me and left me, and I was fired from my job."

The gatekeeper then removed the mask she had been wearing. The woman gasped and fell back on her bed. She couldn't believe her eyes. The gatekeeper was a mirror image of herself.

"Are you ready?" the gatekeeper asked. "Are you ready to forgive and forget? I really want to set us free, you know. I want us to join the other singers."

How many times have we kept ourselves in a prison of bitterness and hate, not willing to forgive and forget the wrongs against us? It's the hurtful past that holds us back. Healing and growth comes when we forget those things that are behind and reach forward to those things that are ahead.

Did you also know that growth may come about by letting go of things we cherish? Sometimes what presently works for and is enjoyed by us may hinder our future goals and accomplishments. Think about the Apostle Paul's situation. Paul, who was well respected among his peers, abandoned his privileged lifestyle and embraced a life of serving Christ. Many lives were changed for the better because of this man, who was once embittered against Christians, did a 360° turn-around. On the surface, it may seem to have cost him much. However, Paul recognized the more noble prize, fixed his eyes on Jesus, and reached for the upward call of God.

Prayer

Father, forgive me for holding onto bitterness and hate. Forgive me for holding onto anything that would keep me from the full release of Your love and power in my life. Help me to forget those things that are behind and to press forward toward those things that are ahead. I press toward the goal for the prize of the upward call of God in Christ Jesus.

Evening

Brightness of His glory: Full of brilliance, splendor, luster, radiance, and effulgence. The manifestation of His glory.

> The Son is the radiance of God's glory and the exact representation of his being, sustaining all things by his powerful word. After he had provided purification for sins, he sat down at the right hand of the Majesty in heaven.
>
> (Heb. 1:3)

Diadem of beauty: Encircling crown of beauty.

> In that day the Lord Almighty will be a glorious crown, a beautiful wreath for the remnant of his people.
>
> (Isa. 28:5)

Philippians 3:13–14

____

____

____

____

Exercise

What is it that you need to forget and leave behind? What are the things you need to embrace? What can you do to let go of the past and embrace what God has for you?

Journal Exercise

Promise:

Principle:

Application:

DAY 37

God Has Plans For Me

Morning

For I know the plans I have for you declares the Lord; plans to prosper you and not to harm you; plans to give you a hope and a future.

(Jer. 29:11)

A New Future

"What's the use?" Doris asked. "I'll never be able to use my legs again. I just might as well be dead!" she cried.

"Doris, you still have so much to offer. Your students will be devastated if you don't return to school. They all love you," her sister said.

"I can't think about anyone or anything right now!" Doris screamed. "I want to be left alone."

Just then her phone rang.

"Aren't you going to answer it?" her sister asked.

"I don't want to talk with anyone!"

Joan picked up the phone.

"Hello? Oh, Susan! How are you? No, she's not able to talk to anyone right now. All right, hold on," said Joan. "Doris, this is the fourth time she's called. You've got to speak to her."

Doris turned her head away and said nothing.

"I'm sorry, Susan. Maybe you can try another time," Joan said.

An hour later there was a knock at the door.

"May I help you?" asked Joan.

"I know we've never met in person, but I am Susan, Ms. Gatlett's student. I brought along some of her other students. We just want to see her."

"Come in," said Joan. "It may take me awhile to bring her in, but be patient."

Joan knocked on Doris' bedroom door and entered without waiting for a response.

"Doris, some of your students are here. You must come out."

"No, I can't see anyone. I can't walk. I look hideous. I . . ." her voice trailed off as she heard the song that she wrote being played. The music was coming from beyond the door. When it stopped, she cried. A few minutes later, there was a knock on the door.

"Ms. Gatlett, did you hear your song?" asked the voice. "Camille's cousin is a producer, and we sang it to him one day. He asked us to do a demo because he thinks it has the potential to be a hit. I hope you don't mind, but we all felt this was a chance you shouldn't miss. We talked with your sister about it when you were in the hospital. She thought it was a great idea. What do you think? Ms. Gatlett, Ms. Gatlett?"

At that moment Doris felt a warm rush fill her body. She was overwhelmed by what her students did. All you could hear through the house were her sobs.

There are so many of God's promises to get excited about. Jeremiah 29:11 is one of them. God promises to give us a bright future in this life and into eternity. Let us give Him permission to plan and have His way in our lives. The rewards are awesome!

Prayer

Father, I thank You for Your plans for me. Even before I was conceived, You knew me and had plans to keep me on a straight and right path. Your plans for me include living life abundantly—full of rich, spiritual treasures, as well as material provisions. Your Word says that many plans are in a man's heart, but Your purposes will prevail. Please continue to direct my steps that Your purposes will prevail. Thank You, Lord, for the rich future You have in store for me in Your blessed kingdom.

Evening

Author and finisher of our faith: Jesus, the One who leads us on a path that brings us to conviction, understanding, and commitment of His Ways through His Word, His Fellowship, our personal experiences, and our surrender to Him.

Jeremiah 29:11

___

___

___

> Let us fix our eyes on Jesus, the author and perfecter of our faith, who for the joy set before him endured the cross, scorning its shame, and sat down at the right hand of the throne of God.
>
> (Heb. 12:2)

Exercise

Write down three promises God made regarding your future. What is your responsibility in allowing those promises to be fulfilled in your life? What can you do to allow those promises to manifest in your life?

Journal Exercise

Promise: ______________________________

Principle: ______________________________

Application: ______________________________

DAY 38

Relax, You Will Grow Up

Morning

> . . . Being confident of this very thing, that He who has begun a good work in you will complete it until the day of Jesus Christ.
>
> (Phil. 1:6 NKJV)

The Finished Portrait

"Kevin, we'll be late for the movies!" George hollered. There was no response. "Kevin?" George screamed, "Kevin?" Still there was no response.

George made his way into the far room of the basement and found Kevin busy working on his latest painting.

"Kevin, didn't you hear me calling you?" George asked, irritated.

"Sorry, George, but I can't break away now. I'm almost finished with the painting."

"Man, we're going to be late!" George shouted. When he looked at the picture, he became silent. "Man, I had no idea you were this good. This is great!" he exclaimed.

"Okay, okay," Kevin said. "I'll wash my hands and we can get going."

"No really, man, your work is great—more than great," George said. Kevin smiled.

"All right. I'll finish it when we get back," he said.

"No, man," said George. "I'll just watch you instead. We'll see the movie tomorrow."

The fact that we are alive signifies that God is not finished with us yet. We are like an incomplete portrait. However, as long as we breathe, we still have opportunity for God to work in us. When we turn our lives over to Him, we don't immediately become perfect people. We have to go through a process in maturing. We are matured through applying God's principles and precepts in our everyday experiences. We can become discouraged when we don't realize that He who has begun a good work is faithful to complete it. Be encouraged and know that Your God will complete that which He has started.

Prayer

Lord, I am thankful that You will complete that which you have started in me. You are the faithful God. When I am discouraged, remind me to encourage myself in Your Word just as King David did. I am glad that You are the God who will never give up on me.

Evening

The Potter: The one who forms and determines.

Yet, O Lord, you are our Father. We are the clay, you are the potter; we are all the work of your hand.

(Isa. 64:8)

Does not the potter have the right to make out of the same lump of clay some pottery for noble purposes and some for common use?

(Rom. 9:21)

Philippians 1:6

____

____

____

Refiner and purifier: The one who fuses, extracts, clarifies, expiates, and cleanses.

> He will sit as a refiner and purifier of silver; he will purify the Levites and refine them like gold and silver. Then the Lord will have men who will bring offerings in righteousness, and the offerings of Judah and Jerusalem will be acceptable to the Lord, as in days gone by, as in former years.
>
> (Mal. 3:3–4)

Exercise

What tools does God provide for our maturing? How do you use the tools God has given you? How have you reacted to God's refining process in your life? What can you do to allow God to mature you?

Journal Exercise

Promise: ____________________

Principle: ____________________

Application: ____________________

DAY 39

How to Receive Grace and Favor

Morning

> For the Lord God is a sun and shield, the Lord bestows [present] grace and favor and [future] glory . . . No good thing will He withhold from those who walk uprightly.
>
> (Ps. 84:11 AMP)

Following the Star

Did you know that the sun is actually a star? This star is the dominant body of the solar system around which the earth and other celestial bodies revolve. These celestial bodies consist of planets (nine major and sixty planetary satellites), asteroids, comets, and moons. Without the sun, the earth would be a dead planet, having no life.

Did you know that food is created through a process of photosynthesis in which the sun plays a major role? Specifically, the chlorophyll in plants absorbs the sunlight, en abling carbon dioxide from the air to bond with water and minerals from the soil to create food. This process causes much needed oxygen to be released into the air. We all need oxygen to breathe. The sun's rays give us warmth. We also need the sun to assist in healing.

Likewise, the Son of Righteousness, the Bright Morning Star, gives us good things—healing, freedom, power, and eternal life. Because of Jesus' righteousness, we are made righteous. Even though we are made righteous through Jesus, God instructs us to live our lives in a way that is good, honorable, and pleasing before Him. The Bible records Jesus as a man who knew no sin. We have a beautiful Savior who provides the blueprints for living. He promises good things—grace, favor, and glory—to those who follow His way.

Prayer

Lord, You are my Bright Morning Star, the Son of Righteousness, who knew no sin. Thank You for being my sun and shield. I choose to follow Your ways. The Bible tells me that You became a curse to redeem me from the curse of the law. Thank You, Lord. Your sacrifice resulted in my receiving good things: protection, healing, freedom, power, grace, favor, glory, and eternal life.

Evening

Sun and shield: Luminary God and protector.

Psalm 84:11

___

___

___

The Father of lights: The Father of celestial illumination, radiant brilliancy.

Every good and perfect gift is from above, coming down from the Father of the heavenly lights, who does not change like shifting shadows.

(James 1:17)

Bright Morning Star: The sun of righteousness; self-luminous One; the glory of the resurrected life who will govern the earth in peace.

> I, Jesus have sent my angel to give you this testimony for the churches. I am the root
> And the offspring of David, and the bright Morning Star.
>
> (Rev. 22:16)

Exercise

The above titles describe God as having illumination and brilliance. Why do you think those adjectives are ascribed to God? What good things does God refer to in Psalm 84:11? What is required of you in order to receive those good things?

Journal Exercise

Promise: ____

Principle: ____

Application: ____

DAY 40

I Will See God

Morning

For I know my Redeemer lives, and that in the end he will stand upon the earth. And after my skin has been destroyed, yet in my flesh I will see God.

(Job 19:25–26)

The Look of Peace

My father suffered for many years with various health problems before he passed away. After being rushed to a hospital one day, he was diagnosed with a stroke. Initially, the stroke resulted in my father's inability to use his left arm. Though he could only walk with help, he had the use of both legs. He was told therapy would make his legs stronger.

My father started therapy and decided he did not like the exercises. He did not want to deal with the pain. Therapy ended, however, when the therapist determined additional therapy would be of no help to him. He advised that we walk Dad several times a day to keep his legs strong. My mother suffered from arthritis and was weak herself, so walking Dad would have made her condition worse. Eventually, moving and walking became too painful for Dad, and he lost the use of his legs. Some months before his death, doctors talked of amputating one of his feet due to its lack of blood circulation.

The doctors attempted to perform an angioplasty, but the arteries were not strong enough for the procedure because a portion of his arteries had deteriorated. Adding to all of those problems, my father had several heart attacks before and after his stroke. He also experienced seizures as a result of the stroke.

Given all that, what do you think my father was holding onto? He believed the promise that Jesus would redeem that "old, decaying body." My father looked forward to the day when he would see Jesus face to face. That was the hope and the light he clung to in his dark circumstances. Admittedly, he gave up on this life. He experienced depression, but what gave him joy and peace was the fact that "though his flesh be destroyed, yet with his eyes he would see God." You see, he knew his Redeemer lives.

On August 2, 2001, my father died peacefully in his sleep. My mother said it was the most peaceful look she had ever seen on my father's face. I admit, he looked wonderful—so wonderful that I believe he saw his angels escorting him into the presence of God. Looking at my father gave the family comfort that he was granted the desire of his heart—to see his Redeemer with his own eyes.

The Bible says we have a Friend who has redeemed us from anything harmful that befalls us. His life in exchange for our life. If we die by a bullet, in a car or airplane accident, if we die by fire or by means of an illness, there awaits a loving Father with a host who have gone ahead of us. No matter what happens to our bodies on this earth, redemption requires that we see God face to face. Our flesh will be destroyed by some means, but it's good to know that our eyes shall behold Him—the One who in the end will reign on the earth.

Prayer

Lord, You are my Redeemer, and I count that a great blessing. *I know I can never repay You* for all You've done for me. Please never let me forget the sacrifice You made for me. I am thankful, Jesus, that You will reign on the earth, and with my own eyes, I will see You.

Evening

Redeemer: The one who buys up or purchases; the one who releases, delivers, and frees from the power and presence of sin, bondage and death by paying a ransom.

Job 19:25–26

May the words of my mouth and the meditation of my heart be pleasing in your sight, O Lord, my Rock and my Redeemer.

(Ps. 19:14)

Our Redeemer—the Lord Almighty is his name—is the Holy One of Israel.

(Isa. 47:4)

For there is one God—and one mediator between God and man, the man Christ Jesus, who gave himself as a ransom for all men—the testimony given in its proper time.

(1 Tim. 2:5–6)

Exercise

What has the Lord redeemed you from? How has that affected the relationships around you? How have you shown gratitude to the Lord for your redemption?

Journal Exercise

Promise:

Principle:

Application:

DAY 41

God Has Not Rejected Me

Morning

> I have chosen you and have not rejected you. So do not fear, for I am with you; do not be dismayed, for I am your God. I will strengthen you and help you; I will uphold you with my righteous right hand.
>
> (Isa. 41:9b–10)

A Chosen Star

Have you seen the television show called *Pop Stars*? This show conducts talent searches for promising young stars who want to make it in the entertainment business. On one of the shows, a young lady was chosen as a finalist for the *Pop Stars* singing group. She explained to some of the judges that she was not beautiful, and she was very insecure about her own capabilities. The judges saw past what she considered as hindrances and, to her surprise, chose her to be in the singing group. She was not dismissed as being invaluable or insignificant. The judges felt she had a lot to offer and that she was a good fit for the group.

The word chosen lets you know how special and important you are to God. He could have looked the other way when you were born. He could have let you go through life without Him ever approaching you. God says that you are worthy of His attention, love, and protection. Just as those judges in the *Pop Stars* talent search did not dismiss the young lady who thought she was not beautiful, God says He has not rejected you as a worthless or insignificant person. He loves you so much that a glorious future is prepared for you. God says that His heart is filled with passion and desire to help, and His security is yours for the asking.

Prayer

Father, I thank You for choosing me and not rejecting me. Thank You for adopting me into Your family. Let Your strong arms help me. Hold me up in any situation. Thank You for counting me worthy and for taking away all my fears. I place myself in Your more than capable hands.

Evening

Spirit of adoption: The one who legally takes and raises another as his own child.

Isaiah 41:9b–10

____

____

____

____

> For you did not receive a spirit that makes you a slave again to fear, but you received the Spirit of sonship. And by him we cry, "Abba, Father."
>
> (Rom. 8:15)

Author of eternal salvation: Jesus is the Source of everlasting deliverance as a result of His finished work on the cross.

> And having been perfected. He became the author of eternal salvation to all who obey Him.
>
> (Heb. 5:9 NKJV)

Exercise

What is the significance of being adopted by God? How did Jesus' mission on earth have an impact on your being adopted by God? What does this tell you about God's nature? Since you are legally adopted and chosen by God, how should you view your relationship with your heavenly Father? What are your entitlements from that relationship?

Journal Exercise

Promise: ______________________________

Principle: ______________________________

Application: ______________________________

DAY 42

God Has Prepared Good Things for Me

MORNING

Eye has not seen, nor ear heard, nor have entered into the heart of man, the things which God has prepared for those who love him.

(1 Cor. 2:9 NKJV)

Another Chance

She had been tired from the trip. It took her over three days to reach her destination by train. It wasn't going to be easy to start her life all over again. She had given up so much even though much had been snatched away from her. Her business partner and trusted friend of twenty years sold their company from right under her nose, and she was left with nothing.

"I should have seen the signs," she said over and over again.

Now she was back home, tired, but ready to put the past behind her. She had slept long and hard. It was the best sleep she had had in about six months. The house was quiet when she awoke. "Mom, Dad?" she called out. There was no answer.

She freshened up a bit and made her way downstairs. When she opened the dining room door, the table was set. Baskets containing fresh fruit, bagels, yogurt, and other goodies caught her eye. In the middle of the food was an envelope with her name on it.

When she opened it, tears began to cascade down her cheeks. A card inside contained a check in the amount of $50,000. The card read, "We love you. Welcome home. Yours for a bigger and better business. You have our love and support."

Try to visualize the things God has in store for you. Can you imagine the preparations He's made for your every need? Can you imagine the bonuses and surprises God delightfully withholds for the right moment? Can you do it? I know that some of these things may be hard to imagine because we see only dimly. According to God, our finite mind is not able to perceive how great these treasures are. How, then, can we not get excited and fall on our knees with grateful hearts before Him? He has done so much for us all. Just think! The King of all kings has prepared something too wonderful to imagine just for us.

Prayer

Thank You, Father, for all that You have prepared for me. Your Word tells me that I cannot fathom or understand Your holy ways. You said that my eyes have not seen, nor have my ears heard all the good things You have prepared for those who love You. Help me to appreciate what You have done for me. I humble myself before You now and ask for forgiveness for an ungrateful heart. May my heart forever be grateful to You. Lord, I offer up to You a sacrifice of praise as a sweet-smelling aroma to You right now. (Take a minute to praise Him.)

Evening

Preparer of good things: The one who sets up, establishes, allots, arranges, makes and delivers, health, prosperity, value, success, and virtue.

1 Corinthians 2:9

____

____

____

Surety of a better covenant: The guarantor; the security of a preeminent, super-abounding contract.

> Because of this oath, Jesus has become the guarantee of a better covenant.
> (Heb. 7:22)

Exercise

What is the better covenant that God made with man? What does that tell you about Him? What is your response to this better covenant? How have you committed to the covenant God has with you?

Journal Exercise

Promise: ____________________

Principle: ____________________

Application: ____________________

DAY 43

God Supports Me

Morning

For I am the Lord, your God, who takes hold of your right hand and says to you, Do not fear; I will help you.

(Isa. 41:13)

The Unwanted Airplane Ride

My daughter, Maisha, and I waited patiently for the late airplane. We laughed when we saw an orange and purple plane taxi to our gate.

"I've never seen a plane with such loud colors," I remarked.

The airplane was not identified by the airline that booked our flights. The name of a sports team was imprinted on the outside of the airplane.

"Oh my!" I said. "What kind of an airplane is that?"

As the passengers were deboarding, Maisha remarked, "Mom, did you see that short pilot?"

"No," I replied.

We soon started chatting again and after awhile, Maisha exclaimed, "Mom, that pilot is short. He's going to be flying the plane?"

"Maisha," I responded, "it doesn't matter how short he is. It should have nothing to do with his ability to fly that airplane." When we seated ourselves inside the airplane, Maisha continued to talk about the pilot's height. "Maisha, leave that pilot alone," I said.

Then I told her of some pretty scary moments I experienced on different airplanes. I also shared the experiences of others who had encountered frightening situations while flying.

"I'd better stop sharing these awful stories," I said. "We should be focusing on good things. After all, God kept us safe throughout those shaky airplane rides."

About fifteen minutes into the flight the attendants began serving refreshments. Suddenly the airplane shook violently. The frightened flight attendants immediately stopped what they were doing, and one quickly sat on the arm of a nearby seat.

"What's he doing?" she snapped at another attendant, referring to the pilot.

I immediately thought, *What does she mean what's he doing? That doesn't sound too comforting.*

A few minutes later, the plane shook violently again. This time it was worse. It felt like the airplane was going to fall out of the sky. I did not hesitate to call on the name of the Lord and pray out loud. Afterwards Maisha seemed to be somewhat embarrassed, but I didn't care who heard me. I just wanted to make sure my Savior heard.

Then the pilot took us to a higher elevation, which made the ride smoother. When the flight attendants became more comfortable, they began to move around again.

"Was that turbulence?" I asked the flight attendant nearest me.

"Yes!" she snarled.

She then tossed the snack into my lap and quickly proceeded to the rear of the airplane. Obviously she was quite upset.

"You see, Maisha, you should have never talked about that pilot. He must have heard you, and it was pay-back time," I said, trying to lighten the moment.

As I continued to inwardly focus on God, I felt impressed that He wanted me to tell Maisha we would arrive safely. I shared with Maisha what I had sensed from the Lord. Do you know what she asked me?

"How do you know?"

Now I am the first one to tell you, I do not always hear God speaking to me, but I felt reasonably sure He had at that moment.

"It's what I felt the Lord was telling me," I said. "You don't have to worry. He's going to keep us all safe," I told her.

Maisha was still frightened, and I admit I was still feeling somewhat uneasy. But I put my confidence in His Word that "He would give His angels charge over us and we were not to fear because the Lord would help us." Believe me, we both were thanking God for His safe keeping during that trip.

It's easy to get scared when surrounded by unpredictable or unforeseen circumstances. Knowing that God hears, reaches out, and lifts us out of frightening circumstances leaves us with a certainty that we can rely on His help. The challenges and mountains of life will not overcome us, because we have a loving and powerful Father with a strong hand.

Prayer

Father, thank You for Your hand that reaches out to help me at every turn in life. You are my strength and shield. You rescue me when I need You. I will not fear because You help me each day with the problems and cares that I face. I need You more than anyone, and I am grateful for a God like You.

Evening

My supporter: The one who cares, helps, aids, and succors.

They confronted me in the day of my disaster, but the Lord was my support.
(2 Sam. 22:19)

They confronted me in the day of my disaster, but the Lord was my support.
(Ps. 18:18)

Isaiah 41:13

____

____

____

Savior of all men: Deliverer of all men.

> This is a trustworthy saying that deserves full acceptance (and for this we labor and strive), that we have put our hope in the living God, who is the Savior of all men, and especially of those who believe.
>
> (1 Tim. 4:9–10)

Exercise

In what ways do both the Father and the Son help us? What does God want your response to be in the face of fear? How can you acquire and maintain peace during turbulent times?

Journal Exercise

Promise: ____

Principle: ____

Application: ____

DAY 44

No More Distortions

Morning

> For now we see in a mirror dimly, but then face to face. Now I know in part, but then I shall know just as I also am known.
>
> (1 Cor. 13:12 NKJV)

A Clear View

Why does the Bible say we now see dimly in a mirror? Think about it. There is an unlimited amount of information that we don't know about God or His kingdom. We see and understand with our natural minds, but there is a spiritual realm that is too vast for us to truly understand. We can barely glimpse this almighty, omnipotent, omnipresent, powerful Ancient of Days. How can we put information about a never-ending, eternal being into our finite minds and say we know all we need to know about Him? How can we take an eternal being and compact Him into our limited minds? How much can we know of Him during our short existence on earth? Once we step over to the other side of life, then will we see Him clearly. Only then will we know Him in His indescribable glory. Think about it. No more distortions. We have a lot to look forward to.

Prayer

Father, I realize I do have a lot to look forward to. Knowing You in all of Your majesty and glory is a privilege. I am glad that I will no longer see dimly or no longer know in part. Thank You for giving me the opportunity to know You here on earth, and thank You for giving me the opportunity to know You in all of Your glory in Your kingdom.

Evening

Revealer of truth: The one who discloses mysteries and reality.

1 Corinthians 13:12

___

___

___

Spirit of wisdom and revelation: Spirit of understanding, moral insight, intelligence, and mystery.

> I keep asking that the God of our Lord Jesus Christ, the glorious Father, may give you the Spirit of wisdom and revelation, so that you may know him better.
>
> (Eph. 1:17)

Exercise

Who is the Spirit of wisdom and revelation? Why was He given to us? What does Ephesians 1:17 tell us about man? What does Ephesians 1:17 tell us about God? What does 1 Corinthians 13:12 mean to you? What steps are you taking to know God better?

Journal Exercise

Promise: ____________________________

Principle: ____________________________

Application: ____________________________

DAY 45

No More Tears, Grief, or Pain

Morning

Then I heard a mighty voice from the throne and I perceived its distinct words, saying, See! The abode of God is with men, and He will live (encamp, tent) among them; and they shall be His people and God shall personally be with them and be their God. God will wipe away every tear from their eyes; and death shall be no more, neither shall there be anguish—sorrow and mourning—nor grief nor pain anymore, for the old conditions and the former order of things have passed away. And He Who is seated on the throne said, See! I make all things new. Also He said, Record this, for these sayings are faithful—accurate, incorruptible, and trustworthy—and true (genuine). And He (further) said to me, It is done! I am the Alpha and the Omega, the Beginning and the End. To the thirsty I [Myself] will give water without price from the fountain (springs) of the water of life. He who is victorious shall inherit all these things, and I will be God to him and he shall be My son.

(Rev. 21:3–7 AMP)

Harmony At Home

When she opened her eyes, she saw a beautiful botanical paradise all around. There were streams of water that radiated beams of indescribable crystalline colors. Instead of birds chirping, she heard soft, beautiful choruses that seemed to emanate from every tree, every bird, every flower, every rock. The choruses would reach a crescendo and then level out to various melodious praises.

Such music I've never heard before, she thought.

"That's because your ears have never heard music in its purist form," said the voice.

"Who are you?" she asked.

"I believe you know already. Should you close your eyes and open them again?" the voice asked delightfully.

"Oh, yes, I know You. You are my Lord," she said excitedly. "My appointed time was up and now I am finally home. Why, there is absolutely perfect harmony in everything I see and hear. Beauty surrounds me!" she exclaimed. "I feel no pain, neither do I have regrets about anything that has happened in my life. Lord, thank You for keeping Your promise to me. I really am eternally Yours."

We have a guarantee in writing of a future without tears or pain. We can look beyond the present state of affairs. We can look beyond what appears to be hopeless circumstances. Our comfort and security comes in knowing that God, the promise keeper, has recorded this message centuries ago to give us clarity concerning the future. He unequivocally states that He will be with us. This guarantee extends to every person who is victorious. Who are the victorious? Those who allow the Alpha and the Omega to direct, guide, and be explicitly involved in their lives. So rejoice for we have a glorious future.

Prayer

Lord, I look forward to spending eternity with You. What a glorious eternity! My journey here is not in vain for You have been with me all along. I thank You that with You there will be no more tears, no death, and no pain because the old conditions and former order of things will pass away. Thank You, Father, the Alpha and Omega, for living water. Thank You for helping me to be victorious. You are my God and I love You.

Evening

The God of eternity: The God of timelessness.

Then I heard the angel in charge of the waters say: "You are just in these judgments, you who are and who were, the Holy One, because you have so judged."

(Rev. 16:5)

Alpha and Omega: The beginning and the end; One who was and is and is to come.

Revelation 21:3–7

____

____

____

____

Exercise

Why do you think God is called the Alpha and Omega? What does the promise in Revelation 21:3–7 say about man? What does it say about God? What do you have to look forward to? What are you doing in your own life to be victorious and inherit eternal life? Journalize your thoughts.

Journal Exercise

Promise:

Principle:

Application:

APPENDIX A

Names, Titles, and Descriptions of God

Subject	Scripture	Page
Alpha and Omega	Rev. 21:3–7	217
Almighty	2 Sam. 5:9–10; Job 33:4; Amos 5:15; Zech. 4:6; James 5:4	100
Ancient of Days	Dan. 7:21–22	150
Atoning Sacrifice	Isa. 53:11–12; Luke 24:46–47; 2 Cor. 4:8–10; Heb.10:10	158
Author and Finisher of our Faith	Jer. 29:11; Heb. 12:2	183
Author of Eternal Salvation	Heb. 5:9	199
Avenger	2 Sam. 22:48; Esther 7:2–5; Ps. 94:1; Nah. 1:2	104
Baptizer	Matt. 3:11; Acts 22:15–16; Rom. 6:3–4; 1 Pet. 3:21	118
Breath of Life	Rev. 11:11	41
Bright Morning Star	Rev. 22:16	191
Brightness of His Glory	Heb. 1:3	179
Counselor	John 14:16–17a; 14:26; 16:7	136

Subject	Scripture	Page
King Forever and Ever	Isa. 9:6–7	151
Lamb	1 Pet. 1:19–20; Rev. 5:12; 17:14; 19:6-9	50
Lead Warrior	Exod. 14:14; 15:3; Deut. 20:4; 2 Chron. 20:21b–22; 2 Kings 6:16–18	68
Life/Life-giving	John 14:6; 1John: 5:20	40
Lover of My Soul	John 4:13; Rom. 8:38–39	163
Merciful	Deut. 4:31; Neh. 9:31; Ps. 28:6–7	76
Most High	Gen. 14:22; Ps. 7:10	85
My Supporter	2 Sam. 22:19; Ps. 18:18; Isa. 41:13	207
Paraclete	John 14:16–17a; 14:26; 16:7	136
Possessor	Gen. 1:28; 17:8b; Deut. 9:6; Job 41:10b–11; Ps. 105:21	110
Potter	Isa. 64:18; Rom. 9:21; Phil. 1:6	186
Power/Powerful	Ps. 29:4	64
Preparer of Good Things	1 Cor. 2:9	202
Presence	Exod. 33:14; Ps. 89:15–17; Amos 5:14	54
Preserver	Job 33:15–18; Ps. 41:2; 121:3–4, 7; 138:7	154
Protector	Ps. 41:1–2; 91:14	96
Redeemer	Job 19:25–26; Ps. 19:14; Isa. 47:4	194
Refiner and Purifier	Mal. 3:3–4	187
Refuge	Ps. 9:9; 14:6; 31:4; 59:16	26
Rescue	Ps. 18:19	37
Resurrection	John 11:25–26	40
Revealer of Truth	1 Cor. 13:12; Eph. 1:17	212
Reward	Gen. 15:1	46

APPENDIX B

Declarations

Praise

You, O God, are exalted forever.

(Ps. 92:8)

O God, You are very great; You are clothed with splendor and majesty.

(Ps. 104:1)

To the King eternal, immortal, invisible the only God, be honor and glory forever and ever.

(1 Tim. 1:17)

You are the Sovereign Lord, my strong deliverer, who shields my head in the day of battle.

(Ps. 140:7)

Praise the Lord, for You, Lord, are good. I will sing praise to Your name for that is pleasant.

(Ps. 135:3)

I know that the Lord is great, that my God is greater than all gods.

(Ps. 135:5)

Your word, O Lord, is eternal; it stands firm in the heavens.

(Ps. 119:89)

Your laws endure to this day, for all things serve you.

(Ps. 119:91)

Your word is a lamp to my feet and a light to my path.

(Ps. 119:105)

May Your unfailing love be my comfort according to Your promise to Your servant.

(Ps. 119:76)

Glorious and majestic are Your deeds, and Your righteousness endures forever.

(Ps. 111:3)

Praise the Lord. I will extol You, Lord, with all my heart in the council of the upright and in the assembly.

(Ps. 111:1)

Who God Is

You are the Creator of the ends of the earth.

(Isa. 40:28)

You are the Creator of the galaxies and all the starry hosts.

(Isa. 40:26)

My Redeemer is strong. The Lord Almighty is His name.

(Jer. 50:34)

O Lord, I am the clay. You are the Potter; I am the work of Your hands.

(Isa. 64:8)

I know that You are My Redeemer and that You live. At the end You will reign on the earth. Though my flesh be destroyed, yet with my eyes, I will see You, God.

(Job 19:25–26)

You are a sun and a shield.

(Ps. 84:11)

What God Does

Your teaching prolongs my life many years and brings me prosperity.

(Prov. 3:1–2)

The Almighty gives me life.

(Job 33:4)

You avenge me from my enemies.

(Ps. 18:47)

You are a shield around me. You bestow glory on me and lift up my head.

(Ps. 3:3)

You have promised good things to your servant.

(2 Sam. 7:28)

Lord, I am grateful that you do not grow tired or weary.

(Isa. 40:28)

The Lord is gracious to me. He rises to show me compassion. For the Lord is a God of justice.

(Isa. 30:18)

You have plans to prosper me and not to harm me, plans to give me a hope and a future.

(Jer. 29:11)

I thank You that You have begun a good work in me and You will complete it until the day of Jesus Christ.

(Phil. 1:6)

You, Lord God, are a sun and shield. You, Lord, bestow grace and favor and glory. No good thing will You withhold from me because I walk uprightly.

(Ps. 84:11)

God, You will instruct me and teach me in the way I shall go. You will guide me with Your eye.

(Ps. 32:8)

You will fulfill Your purpose for me; Your love, O Lord, endures forever.

(Ps. 138:8)

What Jesus Did for Me

Jesus Christ, You have prepared a place for me.

(John 14:2)

Righteous Jesus, You have justified me by Your sacrifice.

(Isa. 53:10–12)

You justified me and bore my iniquities and made intercession for me.

(Isa. 53:11–12)

I have been made holy through the sacrifice of the body of Jesus Christ.

(Heb. 10:10)

What the Holy Spirit Does

The Holy Spirit makes intercession for me.

(Rom. 8:26)

The Holy Spirit is called to my side to help me.

(John 14:26)

The Holy Spirit leads me into all truth.

(John 16:13)

I am anointed and energized for special service by the power of the Holy Spirit.

(Joel 2:28)

What I Should Do

My heart is steadfast, O God. I will sing and make music with all my soul.

(Ps. 108:1)

I will give thanks to the Lord, for He is good; His love endures forever.

(Ps. 107:1)

Since I have been raised with Christ, I will set my heart on things above, where Christ is seated at the right hand of God. I will set my mind on things above, not on earthly things. For I died, and my life is now hidden with Christ in God. When Christ, who is my life appears, then I also will appear with Him in glory.

(Col. 3:1–2)

As God's chosen, holy and dearly loved, I will clothe myself with compassion, kindness, humility, gentleness and patience. I will bear with others and forgive whatever grievances I may have against another. I will forgive as the Lord forgave me. And over all these virtues, I put on love, which binds them all together in perfect unity.

(Col. 3:12–14)

I will not be anxious for anything, but in everything; by prayer and petition, with thanksgiving, I present my requests to God. And the peace of God, which transcends all understanding, will guard my heart and mind in Christ Jesus.

(Phil. 4:6–7)

I will fix my eyes on Jesus, the author and finisher of my faith, who for the joy set before Him endured the cross, scorning its shame, and sat down at the right hand of the throne of God.

(Heb. 12:2)

I will allow the words of my mouth and the meditation of my heart to be pleasing in Your sight, O Lord, my Rock, my Redeemer.

(Ps. 19:14)

If I remain in Jesus and His words remain in me, all things whatsoever I ask in prayer, believing, I shall receive.

(John 15:7)

I shall do what is right and good in the sight of the Lord that it may be well with me and that I may go in and possess the good land which the Lord promised.

(Deut. 6:18)

I will not be weary in well doing, for in due season, I will reap if I don't faint.

(Gal. 6:9)

Lord, I will find You when I search for You with all my heart.

(Jer. 29:13)

I will wait on the Lord and be of good courage, and He will strengthen my heart.

(Ps. 27:14)

I will delight myself in the Lord, and He will give me the desires of my heart.

(Ps. 37:4)

I will seek first the kingdom of God and His righteousness, and all these things shall be given to me as well. I will not worry about tomorrow.

(Matt. 6:33–34a)

I will forget those things which are behind and reach forward to those things which are ahead. I press toward the goal for the prize of the upward call of God in Christ Jesus.

(Phil. 3:13–14)

The Result of an Abiding Life in Christ

If I remain in Jesus and He in me, I will bear much fruit; apart from Jesus I can do nothing. If anyone does not remain in Jesus, he is like a branch that is thrown away and withers; such branches are picked up, thrown into the fire and burned. If I remain in Jesus and His Words remain in me, I can ask whatever I wish, and it will be given me.

(John 15:5–7)

I am not crushed, in despair, abandoned, or destroyed. I always carry around in my body the death of Jesus so that the life of Jesus is manifested in my body.

(2 Cor. 4:8–10)

I did not receive a spirit that makes me a slave again to fear, but I received the Spirit of sonship, and by Him, I cry, "Abba Father."

(Rom. 8:15)

Forgiveness

For as high as the heavens are above the earth, so great is His love for those who fear Him; as far as the east is from the west, so far has He removed my transgressions from me.

(Ps. 103:11–12)

I will forgive men their trespasses, so my heavenly Father will also forgive me.

(Matt. 6:14)

I will love my enemies, bless them that curse me, do good to those that hate me, and pray for them who despitefully use and persecute me.

(Matt. 5:44)

Love

God sends His love and faithfulness.

(Ps. 57:3)

I thank You that neither death, nor life, nor angels, nor principalities, nor powers, nor things present, nor things to come, nor height, nor depth, nor any other created thing shall be able to separate me from the love of God which is in Christ Jesus my Lord.

(Rom. 8:38)

You are the Shepherd and Overseer of my soul.

(1 Pet. 2:25)

Mercy

The mercy of the Lord is from everlasting to everlasting on those who fear Him, and His righteousness to their children's children, to such as keep His covenant, and to those who remember His commandments to do them.

(Ps. 103:17–18)

You will be very gracious unto me at the voice of my cry; when You shall hear it, You will answer me.

(Isa. 30:19)

Peace

I will hear what the Lord God will speak, for He will speak peace unto His people, and to His saints.

(Ps. 85:8)

The work of righteousness is peace, and the effect of righteousness is quietness and assurance forever.

(Isa. 32:17)

Now, the Lord of peace Himself gives me peace always by all means.

(2 Thess. 3:16)

And the peace of God, which passes all understanding, shall keep my heart and mind through Christ Jesus.

(Phil. 4:7)

Jesus, You gave me Your Word so that in You I may have peace. You said I will have trouble in this world, but that I should be of good courage because You have overcome the world.

(John 16:33)

I will let the peace of God rule in my heart.

(Col. 3:15)

Protection

You are my strength and shield. My heart trusts in You and I am helped. My heart leaps for joy and I will give thanks to You in song.

(Ps. 28:7)

You deliver me in times of trouble. You protect me and preserve my life.

(Ps. 41:1–2)

No weapon formed against me shall prosper, and every tongue which rises up against me in judgment, I shall condemn. This is the heritage of the servants of the Lord, and my righteousness is from You, Lord.

(Isa. 54:17)

Surely God is my help. The Lord sustains me.

(Ps. 54:4)

For God has delivered me from all my troubles.

(Ps. 54:7)

I will cast my care upon the Lord, and He will sustain me. He will never let me fall.

(Ps. 55:22)

In God whose word I praise, in God I trust. I will not be afraid. What can mortal man do to me?

(Ps. 56:4)

God fulfills His purpose for me, rebuking those who hotly pursue me.

(Ps. 57:2–3)

Lord, You will not allow my foot to be moved. You don't slumber or sleep. You preserve me from all evil. You preserve my soul.

(Ps. 121:3–4, 7)

You alone are my rock and salvation. You are my fortress. I will never be shaken.

(Ps. 62:2)

You have chosen me and have not rejected me. So, I will not fear, for You are with me. I will not be dismayed for You are my God. You will strengthen me and help me. You will uphold me with Your righteous right hand.

(Isa. 41:9–10)

Provision

God, you will meet all my needs according to Your glorious riches in Christ Jesus.

(Phil. 4:19)

You are my shepherd; I shall not want.

(Ps. 23:1)

APPENDIX C

Promises

Courage/Strength

Even though I walk through the valley of the shadow of death, I will fear no evil, for you are with me; your rod and your staff, they comfort me.

(Ps. 23:4)

The Lord is my light and salvation—whom shall I fear? The Lord is the stronghold of my life—of whom shall I be afraid?

(Ps. 27:1)

He who dwells in the shelter of the Most High will rest in the shadow of the Almighty. I will say of the Lord, "He is my refuge and my fortress, my God, in whom I trust." Surely he will save you from the fowler's snare and from the deadly pestilence. He will cover you with his feathers, and under his wings you will find refuge; his faithfulness will be your shield and rampart. You will not fear the terror of night, nor the arrow that flies by day, nor the pestilence that stalks in the darkness, nor the plague that destroys at midday. A thousand may fall at your side, ten thousand at your right hand, but it will not come near you. You will only observe with your eyes and see the punishment of the wicked. If you make the Most High your dwelling—even the Lord, who is my refuge—

then no harm will befall you, no disaster will come near your tent. For he will command his angels concerning you to guard you in all your ways; they will lift you up in their hands, so that you will not strike your foot against a stone.

(Ps. 91:1–12)

Fear not, for I am with you, be not dismayed, for I am your God. I will strengthen you, I will help you, I will uphold you with my victorious right hand.

(Isa. 41:10 RSV)

Encouragement

The Spirit of the Sovereign Lord is on me, because the Lord has anointed me to preach good news to the poor. He has sent me to bind up the brokenhearted, to proclaim freedom for the captives and release from darkness for the prisoners, to proclaim the year of the Lord's favor, and the day of vengeance of our God, to comfort all who mourn, and provide for those who grieve in Zion—to bestow on them a crown of beauty instead of ashes, the oil of gladness instead of mourning, and a garment of praise instead of a spirit of despair. They will be called oaks of righteousness, a planting of the Lord for the display of his splendor.

(Isa. 61:1–3)

Blessed are the poor in spirit, for theirs is the kingdom of heaven. Blessed are those who mourn, for they will be comforted. Blessed are the meek, for they will inherit the earth. Blessed are those who hunger and thirst for righteousness, for they will be filled. Blessed are the merciful, for they will be shown mercy. Blessed are the pure in heart, for they will see God. Blessed are the peacemakers, for they will be called sons of God. Blessed are those who are persecuted because of righteousness, for theirs is the kingdom of heaven.

(Matt. 5:3–10)

In the same way, the Spirit helps us in our weakness. We do not know what we ought to pray for, but the Spirit himself intercedes for us with groans that words cannot express. And he who searches our hearts knows the mind of the Spirit, because the Spirit intercedes for the saints in accordance with God's will.

(Rom. 8:26–27)

Humble yourselves, therefore, under God's mighty hand, that he may lift you up in due time. Cast all your anxiety on him because he cares for you.

(1 Pet. 5:6–7)

He will wipe away every tear from their eyes. There will be no more death or mourning or crying or pain, for the old order of things has passed away.

(Rev. 21:4)

Eternal Life

In my Father's house are many rooms; if it were not so, I would have told you. I am going there to prepare a place for you. And if I go and prepare a place for you, I will come back and take you to be with me that you also may be where I am.

(John 14:2–3)

And this is what he promised us—even eternal life.

(1 John 2:25)

But in keeping with his promise we are looking forward to a new heaven and a new earth, the home of righteousness.

(2 Pet. 3:13)

Then I saw a new heaven and a new earth, for the first heaven and the first earth had passed away, and there was no longer any sea. I saw the Holy City, the new Jerusalem, coming down out of heaven from God, prepared as a bride beautifully dressed for her husband. And I heard a loud voice from the throne saying, "Now the dwelling of God is with men, and he will live with them. They will be his people, and God himself will be with them and be their God. He will wipe every tear from their eyes. There will be no more death or mourning or crying or pain, for the old order of things has passed away."

(Rev. 21:1–4)

Faith

Therefore, since we have a great high priest who has gone through the heavens, Jesus the Son of God, let us hold firmly to the faith we profess. For we do not have a high priest who is unable to sympathize with our weaknesses, but we have one who has been tempted in every way, just as we are—yet was without sin. Let us then approach the throne of grace with confidence, so that we may receive mercy and find grace to help us in our time of need.

(Heb. 4:14–16)

Forgiveness

In him we have redemption through his blood, the forgiveness of sins, in accordance with the riches of God's grace that he lavished on us with all wisdom and understanding.

(Eph. 1:7–8)

If we claim to be without sin, we deceive ourselves and the truth is not in us. If we confess our sins, he is faithful and just and will forgive us our sins and purify us from all unrighteousness. If we claim we have not sinned, we make him out to be a liar and his word has no place in our lives.

(1 John 1:8–10)

Frustration

Because the Sovereign Lord helps me, I will not be disgraced. Therefore have I set my face like flint, and I know I will not be put to shame.

(Isa. 50:7)

Being confident of this, that he who began a good work in you will carry it on to completion until the day of Christ Jesus.

(Phil. 1:6)

God's Faithfulness

God, who has called you into fellowship with his Son Jesus Christ our Lord, is faithful.

(1 Cor. 1:9)

No temptation has seized you except what is common to man. And God is faithful; he will not let you be tempted beyond what you can bear. But when you are tempted, he will also provide a way out so that you can stand up under it.

(1 Cor. 10:13)

May God himself, the God of peace, sanctify you through and through. May your whole spirit, soul and body be kept blameless at the coming of our Lord Jesus Christ. The one who calls you is faithful and he will do it.

(1 Thess. 5:23–24)

The Lord is not slow in keeping his promise, as some understand slowness. He is patient with you, not wanting anyone to perish, but everyone to come to repentance.

(2 Pet. 3:9)

Hope

Know that the Lord has set apart the godly for himself; the Lord will hear when I call to him.

(Ps. 4:3)

Wait for the Lord; be strong and take heart and wait for the Lord.

(Ps. 27:14)

Be strong and take heart, all you who hope in the Lord.

(Ps. 31:24)

Fear not, for I have redeemed you; I have summoned you by name, you are mine. When you pass through the waters, I will be with you, and when you pass through the rivers, they will not sweep over you. When you walk through the fire, you will not be burned; the flames will not set you ablaze.

(Isa. 43:1b–2)

So let us not become weary in doing good, for at the proper time we will reap a harvest if we do not give up.

(Gal. 6:9)

And the peace of God, which transcends all understanding, will guard your hearts and your minds in Christ Jesus.

(Phil. 4:7)

So do not throw away your confidence; it will be richly rewarded.

(Heb. 10:35)

Peace

I will lie down and sleep in peace, for you alone, O Lord, make me dwell in safety.

(Ps. 4:8)

I will hear what the Lord God will speak, for he will speak peace unto his people, and to his saints.

(Ps. 85:8)

The work of righteousness is peace and the effect of righteousness is quietness and assurance forever.

(Isa. 32:17)

Now, the Lord of peace himself gives you peace always by all means.

(2 Thess. 3:16)

And the peace of God, which passeth all understanding, shall keep your hearts and minds through Christ Jesus.

(Phil. 4:7 KJV)

You will keep in perfect peace him whose mind is steadfast, because he trusts in you.

(Isa. 26:3)

Salvation

Therefore he is able to save completely those who come to God through him, because he always lives to intercede for them.

(Heb. 7:25)

APPENDIX D

Principles

Anger

In your anger do not sin, when you are on your beds, search your hearts and be silent. Offer right sacrifices and trust in the Lord.

(Ps. 4:4–5)

But I tell you anyone who is angry with his brother will be subject to judgment.

(Matt. 5:22)

In your anger do not sin. Do not let the sun go down while you are still angry, and do not give the devil a foothold.

(Eph. 4:26–27)

Commandments

Anyone who breaks one of the least of these commandments and teaches others to do the same will be called least in the kingdom of heaven, but whoever practices and teaches these commands will be called great in the kingdom of heaven.

(Matt. 5:19)

Therefore everyone who hears these words of mine and puts them into practice is like a wise man who built his house on the rock. The rain came down, the streams rose, and the winds blew and beat against that house; yet it did not fall, because it had its foundation on the rock. But everyone who hears these words of mine and does not put them into practice is like a foolish man who built his house on sand. The rain came down, the streams rose, and the winds blew and beat against that house, and it fell with a great crash.

(Matt. 7:24–27)

Conflicts

Settle matters quickly with your adversary who is taking you to court. Do it while you are still with him on the way, or he may hand you over to the judge, and the judge may hand you over to the officer, and you may be thrown into prison. I tell you the truth, you will not get out until you have paid the last penny.

(Matt. 5:25–26)

But I tell you: love your enemies and pray for those who persecute you, that you may be sons of your Father in heaven.

(Matt. 5:44–45a)

Therefore put on the full armor of God, so that when the day of evil comes, you may be able to stand your ground, and after you have done everything, to stand. Stand firm then, with the belt of truth buckled around your waist, with the breastplate of righteousness in place, and with your feet fitted with the readiness that comes from the gospel of peace. In addition to all this, take up the shield of faith, with which you can extinguish all the flaming arrows of the evil one. Take the helmet of salvation and the sword of the Spirit, which is the word of God. And pray in the Spirit on all occasions with all kinds of prayers and requests. With this in mind, be alert and always keep on praying for all the saints.

(Eph. 6:13–18)

Faith

For this very reason, make every effort to add to your faith goodness; and to goodness, knowledge; and to knowledge self-control; and to self-control, perseverance; and to perseverance, godliness; and to godliness, brotherly kindness; and to brotherly kindness, love. For if you possess these qualities in increasing measure, they will keep you from being ineffective and unproductive in your knowledge of our Lord Jesus Christ. But if anyone does not have them, he is nearsighted and blind, and has forgotten that he has been cleansed from his past sins.

(2 Pet. 1:5–9)

Favor

For the Lord God is a sun and shield; the Lord bestows favor and honor; no good thing does he withhold from those whose walk is blameless.

(Ps. 84:11)

Fear

The fear of man will prove to be a snare, but whoever trusts in the Lord is kept safe.

(Prov. 29:25)

There is no fear in love, but perfect love casts out fear. For fear has to do with punishment, and he who fears is not perfected in love.

(1 John 4:18 RSV)

Forgiving Others

For if you forgive men when they sin against you, your heavenly Father will also forgive you.

(Matt. 6:14)

Forgive as the Lord forgave you.

(Col. 3:13b)

Giving

Be careful not to do your acts of righteousness before men, to be seen by them. If you do, you will have no reward from your Father in heaven.

(Matt. 6:1)

Give and it will be given to you. A good measure, pressed down, shaken together and running over, will be poured into your lap. For with the measure you use, it will be measured to you.

(Luke 6:38)

Do not be deceived. God cannot be mocked. A man reaps what he sows. The one who sows to please his sinful nature, from that nature will reap destruction; the one who sows to please the Spirit, from the Spirit will reap eternal life. Let us not become weary in doing good, for at the proper time, we will reap a harvest if we do not give up.

(Gal. 6:7–9)

God's Faithfulness

I will sing of the Lord's great love forever; with my mouth I will make your faithfulness known through all generations. I will declare that your love stands firm forever, that you established your faithfulness in heaven itself.

(Ps. 89:1–2)

God's Forgiveness

If my people, who are called by my name, will humble themselves and pray and seek my face and turn from their wicked ways, then will I hear from heaven and will forgive their sin and will heal their land.

(2 Chron. 7:14)

Seek the Lord while he may be found; call on him while he is near. Let the wicked forsake his way and the evil man his thoughts. Let him turn to the Lord, and he will have mercy on him, and to our God, for he will freely pardon.

(Isa. 55:6–7)

Judging

Do not judge, or you too will be judged. For in the same way you judge others, you will be judged, and with the measure you use, it will be measured to you.

(Matt. 7:1–2)

Love

Be imitators of God, therefore as dearly loved children and live a life of love, just as Christ loved us and gave himself up for us as a fragrant offering and sacrifice to God.

(Eph. 5:1–2)

And so we know and rely on the love God has for us. God is love. Whoever lives in love lives in God, and God in him. In this way love is made complete among us so that we will have confidence on the day of judgment, because in this world, we are like him. There is no fear in love. But perfect love drives out fear, because fear has to do with punishment. The one who fears is not made perfect in love.

(1 John 4:16–18)

Material Possessions

Do not store up for yourselves treasures on earth, where moth and rust destroy, and where thieves break in and steal. But store up for yourselves treasures in heaven, where moth and rust do not destroy, and where thieves do not break in and steal. For where your treasure is, there your heart will be also.

(Matt. 6:19–21)

Oaths

Again, you have heard that it was said to the people long ago, do not break your oath, but keep the oaths you have made to the Lord.

(Matt. 5:33)

Patience

Wait on the Lord; be of good courage, and He shall strengthen your heart; wait, I say, on the Lord!

(Ps. 27:14 NKJV)

Peace

Consider the blameless, observe the upright; there is a future for the man of peace.

(Ps. 37:37)

The fruit of righteousness will be peace; the effect of righteousness will be quietness and confidence forever.

(Isa. 32:17)

Peace I leave with you; my peace I give you. I do not give to you as the world gives. Do not let your hearts be troubled and do not be afraid.

(John 14:27)

Finally, brothers, whatever is true, whatever is noble, whatever is right, whatever is pure, whatever is lovely, whatever is admirable—if anything is excellent or praiseworthy—think about such things. Whatever you have learned or received or heard from me, or seen in me—put it into practice. And the God of peace will be with you.

(Phil. 4:8–9)

Prayer

If you believe, you will receive whatever you ask in prayer.

(Matt. 21:22)

If you remain in me and my words remain in you, ask whatever you wish, and it will be given you.

(John 15:7)

Sin

But if we walk in the light, as he is in the light, we have fellowship with one another, and the blood of Jesus, his Son, purifies us from all sin. If we claim to be without sin, we deceive ourselves and the truth is not in us. If we confess our sins, he is faithful and just and will forgive us our sins and purify us from all unrighteousness. If we claim we have not sinned, we make him out to be a liar and his word has no place in our lives.

(1 John 1:7–10)

Wisdom

But as for you, continue in what you have learned and have become convinced of. Because you know those from whom you learned it, and how . . . you have known the holy Scriptures, which are able to make you wise for salvation through faith in Christ Jesus. All Scripture is God-breathed and is useful for teaching, rebuking, correcting and training in righteousness, so that the man of God may be thoroughly equipped for every good work.

(2 Tim. 3:14–17)

Witness

But in your hearts set apart Christ as Lord. Always be prepared to give an answer to everyone who asks you to give the reason for the hope that you have. But do this with gentleness and respect, keeping a clear conscience, so that those who speak maliciously against your good behavior in Christ may be ashamed of their slander.

(1 Pet. 3:15–16)

Worry

Therefore, I tell you, do not worry about your life, what you will eat or drink; or about your body, what you will wear. Is not life more important than food and the body more important than clothes? Look at the birds of the air; they do not sow or reap or store away in barns, and yet your heavenly Father feeds them. Are you not much more valuable than they? Who of you by worrying can add a single hour to his life?

(Matt. 6:25–27)

But seek first his kingdom and his righteousness, and all these things will be given to you as well. Therefore do not worry about tomorrow, for tomorrow will worry about itself. Each day has enough trouble of its own.

(Matt. 6:33–34)

Do not be anxious about anything, but in everything, by prayer and petition, with thanksgiving, present your requests to God. And the peace of God, which transcends all understanding, will guard your hearts and your minds in Christ Jesus.

(Phil. 4:6–7)

To order additional copies of

Journey *Through* Peaceful Meditations

Have your credit card ready and call:

1-877-421-READ (7323)

or please visit our web site at
www.pleasantword.com

Also available at: www.amazon.com

Printed in the United States
1143200001B/246-312